The Mugging of Black America

Earl Ofari Hutchinson

AFRICAN AMERICAN IMAGES
1990
Chicago, Illinois

Cover illustration by Harold Carr

Photo credits: William Hall

First edition, second printing

Dedication

First to my Father.
Next, to all those who believe that there is nothing in our
history that should make us victims or victimizers.

Acknowledgments

It gives me great pleasure to thank several friends and colleagues for the kind assistance and constructive criticism they gave me in writing this book. My thanks to: Larry Aubry, Dr. John Quicker, and Attorney Legrand Clegg III. I also wish to extend my gratitude to my publisher Jawanza Kunjufu for believing as he said "there is a larger story here that must be told."

Finally, I must extend heartfelt thanks to my wife, Barbara Bramwell-Hutchinson for her warm encouragement, suggestions, and invaluable assistance in preparing the manuscript.

The Mugging
of Black America

Table of Contents

A guy gets tired of being told what he can do and can't do. You get a little job here and a little job there. You shine shoes, sweep streets; anything... You don't make enough to live on. You don't know when you going to get fired. Pretty soon you get so you can't hope for nothing. You just keep moving all the time, doing what other folks say. You ain't a man no more. You just work day in and day out so the world can roll on and other people can live.

I always think of white folks. They choke you off the face of the earth. They like god. They don't even let you feel what you want to feel. They after you so hot and hard you can only feel what they doing to you. They kill you before you die.

Richard Wright, Native Son

Introduction

The evening shadows had begun to fall as the elderly man pulled into the carport of his apartment building. Before he could turn off the ignition, two young blacks ordered him out of his car at gunpoint, ransacked his pockets and stole his car.

Badly shaken, the man stumbled up the stairs to his apartment, collapsed in the front room gasping: "I've been robbed." Another crime committed by blacks. Another black victim. But in this case the horror of the crime was magnified because the victim was my father.

Just as the terror of crime locked its deadly grip on my family that evening it has also gripped millions of other Americans— especially African-Americans. The familiar sight of young blacks in police cars or spread-eagled on the ground is more likely than not to draw the approving nods of many who demand that police get "tough on the hoods." Crime is America's universal bogeyman, and more often than not that bogeyman has a black face.

In 1989, seventy percent of youths transferred from juvenile correctional facilities to prison were black and felony drug arrests for black males jumped 6,700 percent from 1983. At the current pace, by the year 2000, more than fifty percent of young black males will have served time in prison.(1)

The parade of blacks through America's courts and prisons is the end product of the four hundred year experience of African captivity, slavery, segregation, poverty and unequal justice. The cruelest irony is that the enduring legacy of race and class exploitation has turned African-Americans into both victims and victimizers.

In January, 1990 more than sixty blacks were murdered in Washington, D.C. If the killing rate continues, the black death toll for the city will match the total number of American troops killed in Vietnam from 1960 to 1967. The number of black females murdered between 1980 and 1985 exceeds the number of American casualties (9,500) in Vietnam in 1967, one of the peak years of fighting. A staggering 44,428 black males were murdered between 1980 and 1985—nearly equal the total number of Americans killed during the entire Vietnam conflict. Parents are afraid to attend PTA meetings, some children now wear bullet proof jackets to school, and some schools utilize metal detectors.

It has gotten worse. In 1990, an African-American stands a ten times greater chance of being murdered than a white. These black murder victims are not just cold statistics. Their deaths cause grief and pain to family members and friends. Their deaths stir deep soul searching among African-Americans to find out why men and women in the flower of their youth are killing each other. Murder is not the only threat. Blacks stand:

- A forty percent greater chance of being burglarized than whites.
- A fifty percent greater chance of being robbed than whites.
- A twenty-five percent greater chance of being assaulted than whites. (2)

Beyond the human cost of crime and violence, African-Americans must also pay a huge financial bill. Crime cost Americans an estimated $175 billion in 1988 through lost wages, property damage or loss, gambling, narcotics and legal expenses. For private security equipment alone, Americans spent more than $17 million. Since blacks were hit the hardest, the tab for them came to roughly $20 million or 15 percent of the total. The crack epidemic which has devastated African-American communities also exacts a steep economic toll. If estimates are accurate, one percent of blacks spend roughly $100 weekly to feed their cocaine addiction.

The annual dollar drain from African-American communities is $655 million. (3)

But dollars alone are not the only cost. Crime has built a formidable wall of distrust and division among blacks and prevented many from organizing around the issues of poverty, racism, health, educational neglect, and unemployment. These are the major causes of black crime. As one young black said: "Whitey is smart. He gets the brothers to fight each other, when all the time he's out there behind it." (4)

What the young man may not see is that black crime hands much of the media and many public officials the perfect issue to propagate more myths and stereotypes about African-American values and lifestyles. If the public believes that black neighborhoods are war zones run amok with drugs, gangs and violence, then why push for stronger civil rights laws? Why increase funding for social services, education and job programs? Why support criminal justice reforms?

It is hardly accidental that crime replaced economic fairness and social justice on the table of American politics during the Reagan era. Civil rights? Many Americans were too busy barring their homes, locking their cars, and stockpiling mini-arsenals to care.

By liberally sprinkling news reports with terms such as "black-on-black crime," the press heightens public fears. But when whites kill, rob, rape or sell dope to other whites, it is not called "white-on-white crime." There are no separate categories of crime reserved for Asians and Hispanics when they victimize their own. Creating distinctions for black crime makes it seem sinister, alien and totally divorced from American social and economic trends. As Congressman John Conyers said, "It takes black victimization out of the context of the social and economic roots of crime."

The truth is that most thefts or robberies committed by blacks or whites occur within a few blocks of the victim's home. Most murders are committed by family members, friends or acquaintances. The same holds true for rape. A large number of the rapes stem from dates or casual relationships. Put simply: Segregation which still traps most blacks in ghettos and whites in gilded suburbs or ethnic enclaves insures that blacks target blacks, and whites target whites, they are the closest ones. (5)

But these are facts and facts are often the first casualties of a public haunted by the spectre of black crime. Many public officials pander to the public's fears by trying to outshout, outpolitic and outspend each other to get more prisons, law enforcement personnel and punitive laws.

Between 1979 and 1985, lawmakers increased spending on corrections by thirty-four percent; public defense by twenty-five percent; administrative and prosecution staffs by seven percent; and courts by two percent. In all major cities, there were significant increases in funding for police, weapons, training personnel, and deployment.

The 1990-1991 federal budget allocates an additional $7.8 billion for law enforcement, prison construction, and new judges. President Bush offers proposals to expand the death penalty, give police virtually unlimited power to gather evidence, and severely restrict the number of appeals a prisoner can make, as well as limit the time to make them. Even this wasn't good enough. Unable to pass up a chance to play to the folks in Peoria, Bush accused Congress of dragging its feet on the bill. (6)

The end result of the law and order mania is more: street sweeps, curfews, neighborhood barricades, raids on housing projects, bulldozed homes, motorist stops and license checks in African-American neighborhoods. Draconian tactics to be sure, but many African-Americans applaud them because they are tired of having their houses broken into, their purses snatched or attending funerals for friends or relatives murdered in their homes or on the streets.

They agree with Jesse Jackson "that blacks who prey on other blacks are hoods and should be run out of our neighborhoods." In Washington, D.C., blacks strongly backed a city council approved 90 day curfew on youths under age 18. Even though, D.C. Police

Chief, Maurice Taylor made it clear that "the average victim is 31 and the average perpetrator is over the age of 18."

This imaginary scenario drawn by Andrew Hacker during the 1970s is no longer far fetched: "So let's get it out in the open. According to the 1970 census, New York City has 187,146 black men between the ages of 15 and 29. The only way to make a dent in street crime is by withdrawing the constitutional presumption of innocence from these 187,146 citizens. Within their number, lurk most of the city's criminals. The entire stratum will have to endure harsh and humiliating treatment if the dangerous members are to be ferreted out." (7)

Unfortunately, the weary will find no respite from crime in the tough proposals the media and public scream for, and lawmakers pass, because they still do not answer the question: Why African-Americans have become both victims and victimizers? To present a meaningful answer we must first strip away some accepted notions about crime.

Ronald Reagan once told a group of police officials that "disadvantaged childhoods and poverty stricken neighborhoods" do not cause crime. Reagan blamed crime on the victim, not society. Conservatives, of course, applauded because he spoke their language. Crime, they say, is spawned by, take your pick: deviant family structure, immorality, poor self-esteem, low intelligence, and for some a hint of genetic racial inferiority.

Except for a few poorly controlled or self-serving studies, there is no proof that any of these factors are prime causes of criminal behavior. Still, respected criminologists led by James Q. Wilson, assures the public that the only solution to crime is "incapacitation of the offender." This means long prison stretches and the death penalty.(8)

Many blacks and liberals refute the conservatives by pointing to the gaping disparities in the criminal justice system and society. Crime they say is largely caused by:

—The double standard of law enforcement that results in fewer arrests, lighter sentences, greater media and public sympathy for corporate and white collar criminals. The Savings & Loan scandal is a good example. While prisons bulge with poor blacks and Hispanics more than 1,000 bank and S&L fraud cases involving more than $100,000 each went uninvestigated in 1989. Why? because the Bush administration demanded $1.2 billion to fight drug dealing and street crime but allocated only a paltry $49 million for the Justice Department enforcement of banking industry crimes.(9)

——Assaults on civil rights and affirmative action coupled with severe cutbacks in education, job and skill training programs, welfare, education and social services during the Bush-Reagan era.

——Astronomically high poverty, school drop-out and unemployment rates among blacks.

Former Attorney General Ramsey Clark, probably the most articulate crusader in the liberal camp on crime issues, insists that "Crime incubates in places where thousands have no jobs, where houses are old, dirty and dangerous, where people have no rights."(10)

Later we will look at each of these ideas in more detail. However, these explanations for the crime explosion hit closer to the mark than anything the conservatives put forth. But they still leave many African-Americans with a vague sense that something is missing.

To some, liberal answers sound like more apologies for past wrongs to excuse present inaction. They are right. Crime is a deep structural problem in American society—and black crime cannot be separated from that. In fact, the painful truth is that black crime is a hideous consequence of the savaging of black America. It began with African captivity and slavery and its legacy continues to plague America today.

1

The Legacy
of Slavery

During the course of 2½ hours a reporter watched fifty suspects march past Washington, D.C. Superior Court Judge Morton Berg. All but one of the suspects were black. "There is an odd air about the swift afternoon—an atmosphere like that of British Africa in colonial times—as the procession of tattered, troubled, scowling, poor blacks plead guilty or not guilty to charges of drug possession, drug distribution, assault, armed robbery, theft, breaking in, fraud and arson." The reporter witnessed more than a courtroom scene, he witnessed the legacy of slavery.

The African capture and slavery was one of the greatest crimes in history. Every step along the way during the four hundred years of black captivity was marked by brutality, oppression and death. The separation of a people from their land and roots, and the perpetuation of that oppression, a century after emancipation, placed an indelible stamp on African-Americans. They were left in a political and social no-man's land, with no democratic rights and at the whim and mercy of a hostile white society.

Other ethnic minorities suffered intense color and class oppression, but they did not suffer the legacy of slavery. And it is that legacy which still casts a deep shadow over American society today.

Africans learned much from that legacy. They learned that materialism, greed and violence were distinctly European products. Before the coming of the European slaver, Africans fought wars to ward off outside religious invaders, protect a chief or Emperor's right to the throne, or to expand a kingdom's territory. The object of battle was almost never to seize gold, trinkets, or other objects. Nor did Africans engage in violence merely to settle personal rivalries, and antagonisms among members of the same ethnic group.

In the Ashanti and Songhay Kingdoms of West Africa, the region from which most African-Americans can trace their roots, land was held communally, labor was co-operative, and goods were shared or bartered for other necessities. These were complex and intricate societies with established systems of aid and support to the women, young, and the sick. Everyone received a share in the crops, or the goods and utensils produced by iron or metal work. The Yoruba "Esusu", for instance, was a centuries-old formal organization for mutual self-help and support.

Kinship groups, the traditional African extended family and plural marriages also were healthy and viable support systems that established and maintained social harmony and cultural cohesion. Since men were the huntsmen, herders, and farmers, plural marriage was a vital necessity. It provided economic stability and protection for women and children. The practice was accepted by men and women. "There were many instances where a first wife welcomed her second, and where both joined to make a place for the third. Indeed, a woman with her savings will often make it possible for a husband to obtain another wife." (2)

Since this largely eliminated family, personal rivalries, or sexual jealousies, crimes such as rape, murder or assault were virtually unknown. Five centuries of European conquest, colonial and neo-colonial rule, did not entirely destroy those social and economic patterns in West African society. Even today few West Africans kill or assault each other in disputes over women, family matters, or an individual's belongings.

Researchers compared homicide rates among ethnic groups in West and East Africa to Philadelphia blacks. The American black murder rate was 600 times greater than the African. The Gisu and Soga of Kenya recorded no acts of homicide, theft, robbery, property or domestic disputes. There were no fatalities that stemmed from personal insults, curses, or jostling. Not only was the African murder rate lower than that of American blacks, it was also lower than white Americans or Europeans. (3)

The European conquest changed power relations within African society. Shrewdly exploiting territorial and ethnic rivalries, the European divided Africans. Commodity exchange and materialism now became attractive incentives for Africans to kill and help capture other Africans. Entire villages were put to the torch, livestock killed, and women raped during slaving raids. Men, women, and children were clamped in chains and herded at gunpoint to the waiting slave ships. Once on board, they were chained, and stacked sometimes three and four abreast on iron cots with little air, water or food. If the Africans protested they were beaten or flogged. Some were hung or tossed overboard as examples to the others.

It was not unusual for captains to lose nearly half their human cargoes during the Atlantic passage. While history does not record exactly how many Africans perished, W.E.B. Dubois guessed that "every slave imported probably represented on the average 5 corpses in Africa or on the high seas." Gustavus Vassa, an African kidnapped and brought to America in 1756, survived and told what he saw on board ship: "Two of the white men held me fast by the hands and laid me across, I think the windlass, and tied my feet, while the other flogged me severely. I have seen some of these poor African prisoners cut for attempting to jump over the side and hourly whipped for not eating."(4)

The Shadow of the Plantation

Africans were not punished simply because they broke the slaver's rules. Punishment was carefully planned to instill terror and to break the African spirit. Slavery required docility. The African had to be reduced to the level of a beast of burden fitted for hard work and treated as a commodity to be bought and sold. Punishment was an intricate part of the dehumanization process designed to accomplish several ends: submission, rigid discipline, inferiority, and dependence. Violence as a means of social control was skillfully implanted by the slavemaster in the African consciousness.

During slavery, the African was confronted with new rules of conduct. Any violation of the Southern slave codes would bring harsh punishment. The African was tried in informal slave courts where the slave owner sat as judge and juror. The admission of evidence, testimony, or cross-examination was not allowed. Guilt or innocence rested on the word of the master.

Slaves could be tried and punished for an endless list of offenses that ranged from malingering to murder. Violence against the master or overseer topped the list. Guilt was automatic and the punishment could be death for this crime.

In every Southern county, whites were deputized and patrolled city streets, roads, swamps, and rivers on the look-out for runaway slaves or any sign of slave misconduct. Blacks were forbidden to assemble, buy, trade or sell goods without white permission. They could not carry firearms, leave the plantation or walk city streets after nine without written consent. They could not practice medicine, or learn to read or write.

Southern legislatures enacted rigorous laws that regulated the conduct of slaves and gave the slavemaster unlimited rights and power. "The power of the master must be absolute," said North Carolina Supreme Court Judge, Thomas Ruffin in 1829.(5)

Defense of slavery was not just a Southern matter. The Federal government was deeply involved in enforcing pro-slavery laws too. The Constitution explicitly directed Congress to call "forth the Militia" and "to suppress Insurrections." The slave states continually reminded federal officials that they were legally bound to aid any state militia in quelling slave revolts. Under Article IV Section 2 of the Constitution, federal officials also were obligated "on Demand of the executive authority of the State" to return anyone "who shall flee from Justice." For the slave states this meant only one thing, runaway slaves were criminals and the Federal government must return them to the South.

The U.S. Supreme Court did its part to make sure federal officials understood their responsibility under the law. In separate rulings in 1842 and 1850, it upheld the Fugitive Slave Act of 1793. With the Dred Scott decision in 1857, the Court removed any lingering doubts as to the legal rights of blacks. Chief Justice Roger Taney came right to the point: blacks "have no rights which whites are bound to respect."(6)

The Taney edict included free blacks as well. In Massachusetts, immediately prior to the Civil War, one out of six prisoners were black, they were one seventy-fourth of the population; in New York, one out of four prisoners were black, they were one thirty-fifth of the population; in Pennsylvania, one out of three prisoners were black, they were one thirty-fourth of the population.

The system of law and power that controlled the slaves and free blacks had another damaging consequence. It did not punish crimes committed by blacks against other blacks the same way it did crimes against whites. A slave killing another slave was frowned on only because it meant a loss to the master of valued property. But the master would not demand retribution or prescribe a lengthy jail term for the culprit. The loss of the slave's labor would further damage his financial investment.

Theft, assault, or even rape were generally ignored as long as they did not hamper labor or production on the plantation. One planter said that he did not interfere with his slaves "in any way further than is necessary for the good of his interests." Many masters did not stop at benign neglect; they actually encouraged their slaves to get drunk, carouse, engage in illicit sex and fist fights. The planter reasoned that if the slaves took out their anger and frustrations on each other, they would not think of rebelling or running away.

Black abolitionist leader Frederick Douglass told of his experience: "I have known slaveholders resort to cunning tricks, with a view of getting their slaves deplorably drunk. The usual plan was to make bets on a slave that he could drink more whiskey than any other, and so induce a rivalry among them for the mastery in this degradation."(7) Slaves quickly learned what was acceptable behavior and what would bring punishment. They also observed the moral behavior of whites. They noted that alcohol and tobacco consumption, adultery, wife and child beating, theft, and fighting were common practices among many whites. Historian Herbert Gutman confirms that Africans did indeed "adapt to their circumstances" and "learn 'conventional' New World social practices from slave-owning and non-slave-owning whites."(8)

The slaves often lived and worked in close proximity to the poor white farmers and laborers. They saw that violence was part of their way of life. These "lower class" whites were just as likely to settle their disputes with guns. Blood feuds were so common among them that the South evolved a powerful quasi-militarist tradition that carries over to the present day. The murder rate in the South is consistently higher than the rest of the country.

While the Civil War ended chattel slavery, it did not end the systematic terror and violence that had entrapped blacks. The few political gains blacks made during Reconstruction were soon wiped out as the former planters regained control of state governments. The old slave codes quickly gave way to the new black codes. Blacks were arrested and jailed for many of the same offenses as during slavery.

No longer a commodity to be protected by the master, blacks stood naked before the cruelty of Southern law and vigilantism. In 1883, the Supreme Court again stepped in on the side of Southern law. It ruled the Civil Rights Acts of 1866, 1871, and 1875 unconstitutional thus putting severe restrictions on the Federal government's use of the police powers inherent in the anti-slavery 14th and 15th Amendments to protect blacks.

Southern states could now make and enforce any laws they

saw fit without federal interference. If a black was murdered by whites and local officials refused to arrest and indict the assailants, the only legal recourse for federal officials was to bring charges against them for violation of the individual's civil rights. It was a cumbersome, time consuming and ultimately futile process that few federal officials cared to try. For blacks the law became a no-win situation.

The Klan, White Knights and other racist groups unleashed a wave of terror against blacks under the guise of protecting property, womanhood, and the Southern way of life. Between 1880 and 1900, more than 2,500 blacks were lynched. By the start of World War I, the number had grown to more than 4,000. (9)

Crimes were now more closely tied to the economic status of blacks. The very poverty that blacks were relegated to because of the broken Reconstruction promises of land and political rights became in itself a crime. Blacks accused of vagrancy, theft, or disorderly conduct were jailed, sent to work gangs, or hired out as contract laborers. Throughout the South, peonage laws were a thinly disguised system of indentured servitude used to supply farmers and big landowners with cheap (or free) black labor.

The laws were little more than warmed over versions of the old slave codes used to control free blacks. As early as 1787, Southern states enacted laws compelling free blacks to be sold at auction for committing crimes. In 1831, the North Carolina state legislature broadened the definition of crime to include inability to pay fines. As punishment, free blacks were hired out to local landowners to "work off" their fines.

After Reconstruction, convict leasing became the standard practice. Sheriffs and municipal courts had sweetheart arrangements with local farmers and landowners who paid the fines of black prisoners in return for their labor. By 1879, ninety percent of the 1,200 felony convicts in Georgia were black. This percentage would remain unchanged for the next thirty years. In North Carolina, ninety-two percent of the 1,200 prisoners in state prisons were black.

For those who didn't have their fines paid or weren't jailed there was the chain gang. Mostly black convict labor built the ditches, roads, bridges, tunnels, waterways in North Carolina, South Carolina, Georgia, Mississippi, and Alabama. The system worked well for the ruling whites who made the laws, and determined who would be arrested and jailed. They used law and power to suit any situation that demanded cheap black labor. To ensure that black labor was docile and plentiful, Southern courts routinely slapped black offenders with jail sentences two to three times as long as those received by Whites.(10)

Where is the Promised Land?

The segregated South had forced blacks to bond together in family, religion and community. Blacks visited each other's homes, they nursed the aged and sick, and helped raise each other's children. They patronized black grocery stores, barber shops, and beauty parlors and bought insurance from blacks. They were buried by black funeral parlors and regularly participated in church activities.

Even though the all-black schools were mostly one room tar shacks, with tattered second hand textbooks, poor lighting, and no heat, teachers and students began every school day singing James Weldon Johnson's "Lift Every Voice and Sing," the Negro National Anthem. They were taught to be proud of the deeds and accomplishments of black heroes like Booker T. Washington, George Washington Carver, Frederick Douglass, and Harriet Tubman.

Segregation also blurred the social and economic class divisions among blacks. Black doctors, lawyers, educators, and business persons lived next door to black janitors, maids and factory workers. These professional men and women served as examples of black achievement. Young blacks could strive to emulate their success.

Men attended lodges where they discussed politics and traded information about business and crop prices. Women formed auxiliaries and sewing circles. People kept each other apprised of social and personal news and were aware of the significant events in the community. When a friend or neighbor caught a young black stealing or fighting, they would reprimand him on the spot and report it to the parent.(11)

I still remember the times in the small hamlet of Clarksville, Missouri, where I spent my boyhood summers. My grandmother would be waiting at home with a leather belt for me after she got word from a friend or neighbor of my misbehavior. She and other parents encouraged the neighbors to report any misdeed and reprimand each other's children. Despite the intense racism and poverty in small Southern communities, religion, social and family life stabilized black neighborhoods and minimized crime. Even with the blatant racial bias of Southern police and courts, the rate of black convictions for murder, robbery, and arson was lower among Southern blacks than blacks in the North before World War II.

All black towns in the South where white control was at a minimum had the lowest crime rates. Mound Bayou, Mississippi did not record a single murder during the 1920s. Boley, Oklahoma had the lowest crime rate in the state during the 1940s. The picture drastically changed when white administration and law took over.(12)

For decades, murder and theft were virtually unknown among the 8,000 black residents of St. Helena, a South Carolina sea island town. About three persons yearly committed offenses severe enough to go to trial. The social and economic life of St. Helena revolved around a tight-knit network of businesses, farms, and churches. Islanders settled disputes through their "praise house" system. It worked like this. If a man was injured in a fight, as punishment the assailant would either agree to work on the injured man's farm to compensate him for the crops or the work time he lost from the fields.

In 1930, wealthy whites discovered the sandy white beaches of St. Helena. They bought and cleared land, constructed bridges and roads, and built pricey resorts and homes. For the first time, white police began patrolling St. Helena streets. Whites ignored the "praise house" system and made arrests for all violations of the law. The age-old traditions of the Island were shattered. Within a few years, the crime figures for St. Helena matched those of the mainland.(13)

To escape the violence and terror, blacks fled in droves to Chicago, New York, Detroit, Philadelphia, and other Northern cities. Between 1900 and World War I, more than five million blacks left the Deep South. The North was the promised land of opportunity and hope. But the promise of the promised land quickly faded.

The newcomers were packed into crowded slums, charged high rents, excluded from unions and relegated to the dirtiest and most menial jobs in industry. The North transformed the mostly poor, underemployed and unemployed rural Southern black men and women into mostly poor, underemployed and unemployed urban Northern black men and women. "They do not escape jim-crow; they merely encounter another, not-less-deadly variety," wrote James Baldwin, "They do not move to Chicago, they move to the southside; they do not move to New York, they move to Harlem. The pressure within the ghetto causes the ghetto walls to expand, and this expansion is always violent."(14)

Although there were no "colored only" signs in the North, the barriers that excluded blacks were just as rigid. Their experience was totally different from the European immigrants. The first generation immigrants would also pack city slums and ghettos. They would also suffer neglect and discrimination. They would turn to crime as a quick means for social and economic uplift. But they were white. Their children and grandchildren would use education, and their ethnic network of social and political ties to move into mainstream business and the professions. For blacks, color and caste made assimilation difficult.

The NAACP was in its fledgling years and still largely confined to legal and court actions. The black masses remained trapped in the slums with no respite from the daily insults, Jim Crow living conditions and racial abuses. Their frustrations and tensions grew. In the North, as in the South, they had no outlet to release their anger and aggression against whites. Assaults or murders of whites would bring long prison or death sentences. In Richard Wright's *Native Son*, Bigger Thomas tries to make Max, his white lawyer, understand that it is hopeless to expect leniency from the law for a black man who murders a white:

Mr. Max, it ain't no use in you doing nothing!

Do you really feel that way, Bigger?

There ain't no way else to feel.

I want to talk to you honestly, Bigger. I see no way out of this but a guilty plea. We can ask for mercy, for life in prison.........

I'd rather die!

Don't you want to fight this thing?

What can I do? They got me. (15)

Blacks could only victimize other blacks and not be harshly punished by white law. Theft, assaults, rapes, drug addiction, and murders increased in numbers and became more widespread as urbanization broke down the traditional social cohesion of family and community.

By World War II, the social and cultural bonds of the St. Helenas and other rural Southern black communities were quickly forgotten in the North. Competition replaced co-operation, tensions and frustrations grew, and the social and economic distance among blacks widened. A newly arrived Southern migrant bemoaned the lost sense of community: "When I was in the South, I was always helping people, but I haven't been doing any of that work up here. People now crushes me a lot, but I don't say anything. I just go off and cry."(16)

The Painful Emergence of the Black Underclass

There were plenty of reasons for black migrants to cry. During the war, more than two million blacks had migrated to Chicago, Detroit, New York and Philadelphia lured by the promise of war time jobs in aircraft and auto factories. As the resentments of many whites grew, police abuse and vigilante attacks increased. Detroit was the first to explode. Two days of rioting in 1943, left twenty-five blacks and nine whites dead.

Black leaders charged that police were the major instigators of the violence. They refused to arrest white attackers, egged on the crowds and brutalized blacks. Thurgood Marshall, then an NAACP attorney, gave the scorecard: "Yet the record remains: Negroes killed by police—seventeen; white persons killed by police none. The entire record, reads like the Nazi Gestapo." Within weeks, violence broke out in Harlem. Again, police bullets accounted for all the blacks that died.(17)

Black economic fortunes took another sharp downturn with the end of the war. Last hired and first fired once more became the watchword in industry as returning white troops took the jobs in plants and factories that blacks held during the war. The ghettos continued to expand as more blacks from the South continued to flood the Northern cities looking for work. With the lack of jobs and the growing poverty, a black underclass appeared for the first time.

Disconnected from their Southern roots and with no visible opportunities for advancement, the black poor turned to hustling, numbers and theft to survive. Still unable to directly vent their anger and frustration at the oppressive conditions of ghetto life, the black poor took out their bitterness and frustrations on each other. A teen-age Mike Tyson remembered the violence that characterized his early childhood in Bedford-Stuyvesant, "Violence was accepted. It was part of life. You don't want to see anyone get hurt, but I wasn't a stranger to that type of violence."

Loved ones, however, did get hurt because the victims of black violence were nearly always other blacks—not whites. In *Black Skin, White Masks*, Frantz Fanon, recounts this exchange from a play by Jean Genet:

The Negro: I can't shoot white folks.

Lizzie: Really! That would bother them, wouldn't it?

The Negro: They're white folks, ma'am.

Lizzie: So what? Maybe they got a right to bleed you like a pig just because they're white?

The Negro: But they're white folks.

The dialogue between "The Negro" and Lizzie, reveals the dehumanization process that drives young blacks to engage in violent and abusive acts against other blacks. The psychological forces that turns black aggression outward against other blacks is one of the most damaging features of racial and class oppression.

Colonial people display the same pattern of internalized aggression and violence against their own people. The Algerian peasant, under French colonial rule, could not strike back at the French businessman, tax collector, judge or policeman without severe reprisals. He could only take his aggression out on another Algerian. Fanon described the consequences:

"The Algerian, exposed to temptations to commit murder every day—famine, eviction from his room because he has not paid the rent, the mother's dried up breasts, children like skeletons, the building yard which has closed down, the unemployed that hang about the foreman like crows—the native comes to see his neighbor as a relentless enemy."

The African-American experience was worse. While colonial rule was brutal and dehumanizing, the Algerians were not slaves. Algeria was their country, and they were always the majority of the population, not the French. The French could not stamp out the language, culture and social institutions of the Algerians. The Algerian's color was never a badge of shame.(19)

The legacy of slavery drove the psychic pain of oppression deeper within the African-American psyche than colonialism did to its victims. Acts of violence against other blacks became an accepted and safe way to displace aggression. This was not a personality flaw or character aberration of blacks, but a "natural" or "normal" human response. In his pioneer studies on human aggression, Yale psychologist, John Dollard concluded that "aggression is always the result of frustration." Aggression can be especially dangerous because it is not reasoned or controlled. Psychologist Konrad Lorenz found that individuals frequently vent their aggression in spontaneous acts of violence even where there is no immediate overt provocation.

Researchers found that violence can have a spiraling effect. The individual who commits a violent act is not calmed or settled by the release of pent-up aggression. It does not inhibit, but encourages the individual to commit more acts of violence. Studies demonstrated that children encouraged to play aggressive or violent games frequently resorted to violence when they played with other children. Studies of psychiatric patients confirmed that black patients were more likely to feel slights or insults more deeply and vent their anger against other patients. Blacks also were found to be more prone than whites to engage in physical fighting and violence to solve marital problems.(20)

Novelist Claude Brown tells of the legendary havoc from shootings and brawls that blacks wreak on each other on Friday or Saturday nights: "Down home, when they went to town, all the niggers would just break bad. Everybody just seemed to let out their hostility on everybody else. Maybe they were hoping they could get their throat cut then he'd be free from the fields. On the other hand, if someone was lucky to cut somebody else's throat, he done the guy a favor because he'd freed him."(21)

"Subculture of Violence"

Neither the finding of clinicians and sociologists or Brown's fanciful but tragic account of black violence should be interpreted to mean that a "subculture of violence" exists among blacks. Blacks do not kill other blacks in disproportionate numbers for the mere sport of killing.

The "subculture of violence" theory implies this. It creates the impression that violence is somehow in-bred into the black experience. This absolves white institutions of any responsibility for fostering and perpetuating the violent behavior.

Much of the blame for spreading the theory can be placed on the doorstep of Daniel Patrick Moynihan. In his much criticized 1965 report on the black family, Moynihan claimed that the "disorganization" of the black family caused crime, violence, and poverty among blacks. In recent years, black and white theorists have

14

poked gaping holes in his report. They say that Moynihan deliberately ignored the importance of the extended family, alternate male role models, the black middle-class, the increasing graduation rate among blacks, and the presence of the father in nearly seventy-five percent of black homes. (22)

If the policymakers who enthusiastically hailed Moynihan had taken the time to look beneath the surface, they would have seen that black children can receive love, support and attention in even the most "disorganized" homes. This is how Washington, D.C. street robber and ex-convict John Allen remembers his early home life: "My father never lived at home, but my mother, well, me and her were really tight.

My whole family life was good to me as far as feeling for one another like, I love my mother, I love my grandmother and grandfather, my sisters and brothers. I always felt that they felt the same way about me. They have shown me in many ways just how much they care."

There is no evidence that black children who grow up in "disorganized" homes are any more crime prone than white children in the same circumstances. In fact, researchers have found that the rates for juvenile and adult robbery and homicide were slightly higher among white female headed households than among black female headed households.(23)

"Subculture of violence," then, is only another empty term like "black-on-black crime," that sociologists and the media use to separate black violence and victimization from the social and economic causes of frustration, aggression and violence. Black violence is largely a cry of pain, a destructive reaction to the trauma of oppression. The violence is not endemic to blacks. It is endemic to American society. Ralph Ellison's protagonist in Invisible Man shouts:

"You ache with the need to convince yourself that you do exist in the real world, and you strike out with your fists, you curse and you swear to make them recognize you. And, alas, it's seldom successful."

Ellison's character explains why the "Bad Nigger" syndrome has taken on mythic proportions in black stories, songs, and folktales. And been glorified by young blacks. The man of strength who doesn't "take any Sh—" from anybody, who's tough as nails, and will murder anyone who crosses him. Stakolee was just such a black man:

"And I asked the bartender for something to eat,
he give me a dirty glass of water and a tough a__ed piece of meat,
I said, 'Bartender, bartender, don't you know who I am?'
He said, 'Frankly, my man, I don't give a go__am.'
'Bout this time the poor bartender had gone to rest—-
I pumped six of my rockets (bullets) in his mo__erfu__in chest."(24)

While the swagger and tough talk of young blacks sometimes does lead to violence, the Stackolees of the black ghettos represent an extreme, but logical reaction to an oppressive society. The quest by blacks to "make them recognize you," as the Ellison character laments, more often crashes headlong against the bedrock of racism and results in failure, bitterness, and frustration.

"Subculture of Poverty"

Many sociologists rely on the "subculture of poverty" theory to explain black violence. It goes like this.

Supposedly decades of poverty and discrimination have instilled a deviant set of values in black culture that has made crime a natural way of life for young blacks. They are caught in a vicious, unbreakable cycle, learned in the mean streets of the ghetto, and passed on from generation to generation.

Certainly the economic crisis of the Bush-Reagan era has hit African-Americans with devastating impact. Poverty and unemployment rates have soared, while social service, education and job programs have been gutted. But the majority of blacks do not belong to the underclass. Since the post Reconstruction years, there has been class differentiation within black communities. A small but affluent "black bourgeoisie" made up of business persons, doctors, lawyers, educators, and political leaders long formed a social and economic elite among blacks.

Following World War II, their numbers grew. "As the result of the changes in the economic status of the Negro," wrote sociologist E. Franklin Frazier, "the Negro middle-class, has grown in size and acquired a dominant position among Negroes."(25)

The civil rights movement accelerated the growth of the black middle-class. By 1987, thirty-two percent of the 17 million blacks in the workforce had incomes greater than $25,000 and 2.2 percent earned more than $50,000. This was an increase of more than 400 percent since 1970. Black doctors, lawyers, corporate directors and managers, public officials, and mid-range capitalists comprised a prosperous "new black bourgeoisie."

Teachers, government employees, social service workers, skilled blue collar workers, and small businesspersons comprise the black middle-class. Beneath them on the economic ladder is the "working non-poor"—semi-skilled tradesmen, and lower level public employees. Then comes the "working poor," who are the unskilled laborers and day workers.

Two out of three blacks fall into one of these four economic classes. The majority of middle and working class blacks do not move from the black communities. However, they do move to the "better" neighborhoods at the fringe of the ghetto that almost always become all-black because of white flight. Their close presence promotes social stability and positive cultural values within the black community.(26)

Meanwhile, the black elite that do move to white or "integrated" suburbs and send their children to private schools rarely sever their ties completely to the black community. They have family members, friends, and social acquaintances that still reside in the old neighborhood. They interact with them through personal visits, involvement in business, church and social functions.

How does crime fit into the picture? Like other Americans, upwardly mobile black professionals do make the safety and protection of their family members a high priority. However, crime is only one of many reasons for their move to the suburbs. They are equally concerned about the quality of schools, public services and housing. Their "flight," if it can be called that, is to obtain the amenities denied them in the ghetto. The consequence is the lack of role models in the inner city.

The subculture of poverty theorists also fail to recognize that the black poor do not voluntarily choose to live the way they do. The poverty is created from outside through continued denial of employment, education and social services. That is not an individual or "black fault," but society's. It is the rare black welfare mother or unemployed father who does not want their son or daughter to have a good education and career opportunity. They want the same things that the white middle-class wants.

The petty crime that flourishes among the black underclass—hustling, numbers, gambling—has a quasi-legitimacy only because they see this as a way to escape poverty and perhaps fulfill middle-class dreams. Poet and novelist Claude McKay notes that in Harlem, during the 1920s and 1930s, numbers racketeers were respected and played vital roles in the social life of the community. They contributed to businesses, charities, bought real estate and established "legitimate businesses" that provided employment for the residents, "They felt that they had a respectable enough status in the community." For many young blacks the hustlers and numbers racketeers are upwardly mobile success models, not criminals.(27)

One would be hard pressed to find many persons in black (or white) neighborhoods today who would turn down a chance to buy "hot" goods at discount. When they do buy these goods they are giving tacit approval to acts of theft, pilferage or robbery. Large numbers of blacks who looted stores during the riots of the 1960s boasted of their thefts. It can be argued that they were only getting some of the goods that society told them they must have to be successful.

Blacks then, who turn to crime are not in revolt against middle-class norms but distort or "stretch" them to adapt to the circumstances of ghetto life. Poor young black males have become especially adept at this. Even though by all economic indicators black women are at the bottom of the economic barrel, poor young black males are the ones weighted down with the burden of proving their "manhood." They are trapped by society's definition of the successful male as breadwinner and family protector. Since poverty and racism deny many of them the means to legitimately fulfill that role, they will turn to crime in far greater numbers than black women. But whether male or female, the black poor have never been content to wallow in misery or resign themselves to lower standards of material comforts as the "sub-culture of poverty" theory suggests. (28)

The poor young black who deals drugs or commits thefts in the ghetto reflects the violence, poverty, and greed that has shaped much of the African-American experience, past and present. But in a curious way, he aspires to the same wealth and power as the corporate chief executive. In fact, their world's may be different but they are both engaged in the quest for power in capitalist America. Kinship groups, that centered around the traditional African extended family, provided healthy and viable support systems for women and children.

The extended family also served to maintain social harmony and cultural cohesion within village society.(29)

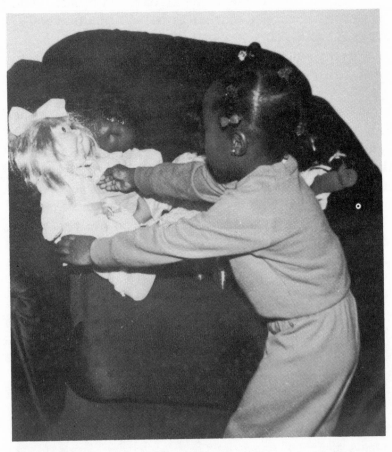

Could it have been that the black children played with white dolls because there were no black dolls?

2

The Quest for Power

"When you has work and some money in your pocket so you can go to the store and buy some meat and bread, then you has the best freedom there is."

An ExSlave

One commentator wryly observed, "Most of the crime in America today is committed by young poor blacks and old wealthy white men." From surface appearances this seems more fact than jest. A 1989 survey by the National Association of Accountants revealed that 87 percent of corporate managers were willing to commit fraud in one or more cases the investigators presented to them.

This should hardly surprise anyone who has even remotely followed the news during the Reagan-Bush years. Numerous studies show that business ethics, never high to begin with in America, sank to an all-time low during this period. The return of 19th century style free-boot capitalism began with a vengeance under Ronald Reagan.

Scandal after scandal within and without the Reagan administration muddied the always tenuous lines between legitimate business and crime. More than 100 Reagan men and women had ethical or legal charges filed against them. The nine Iran-Contra defendants, all Reagan loyalists, were convicted and sentenced for perjury, obstruction of justice and fraud. Government corruption was so great that Time even chided Reagan for being "as permissive as an antiquarian parent over the transgressions of his official family."(1)

But Reagan was more than an "antiquarian parent." His deliberately, lax political conduct sent open signals to the business world. Sixty of the top 100 defense contractors took the cue. They juggled books, submitted phony billings, padded their accounts, and ran up huge cost overruns that cost taxpayers billions. While a few individuals were indicted and fined, the Defense department refused to debar any contractor from doing business.

More than 1,200 Savings & Loan officials took the cue. They used slack regulatory controls to make unsecured loans to friends and family members, payoffs and bribes to developers, and to engage in outright embezzlement of funds. Taxpayers will pay more than $500 billion to clean up the mess.

Wall Street stockbrokers took their cue. The nation watched as dozens were led handcuffed from the New York Stock Exchange accused of insider trading and stock manipulation. The rich and powerful did not complain, they were too busy making money. By the time Reagan left the White House the richest one percent of Americans paid on average, $82,000 less in taxes than before Reagan took office.(2)

Congress tried to convince Americans that it was serious about prosecuting corporate crime and government corruption. It pointed to a rash of post Watergate laws that increased penalties for price-fixing, fraud and ethics violations. But trial judges in nearly all cases still handed out probation, fines, or suspended sentences to white collar crooks.

Prosecutors also promised to crack down harder on suite crime. While they did indict and convict more suite criminals, their numbers paled in comparison to the numbers of black and minority offenders. Prosecutors claimed that they lacked sufficient investigatory and prosecutorial staff, funds, and technical resources to pursue corporations and wealthy individuals who steal. When California District Attorneys were asked how vigorously they went after white collar criminals, 83 percent said they deferred to federal prosecutors, and 54 percent felt that corporate crime was better handled by federal regulators.(3)

Even when an employee is killed or injured as a result of corporate negligence the employer almost never goes to jail. From 1970 to 1988, there were only 14 criminal indictments and ten convictions of employers for violation of the Occupational Safety and Health Administration rules (OSHA). Among 22 European and Asian nations the U.S. had the fourth highest death rate from work-related injuries.

Finally, in 1989, the first employer was jailed for an OSHA violation involving the trench death of a worker. He served forty-five days. The National Association of Manufacturers has mounted a massive lobbying campaign to kill Congressional legislation in 1990 to increase criminal penalties for OSHA violations. The Bush administration joined them in opposing the legislation.(4)

The public outcry against the modern day Robber Barons who work the shady side of the capitalist street is muffled because most Americans perceive that they are only doing what comes natural. American businessmen will lie, cheat and steal to gain property, wealth, and political influence. Economic inequality that makes vast fortunes for a few, at the expense of the many, is deeply embedded in the foundations of the American Republic.

The fifty-five men who met in Philadelphia in 1787 at the Constitutional Convention were either landowners, merchants or slaveholders. They feared the common people. They wanted government to be democratic, but democracy to them must not disturb traditional property and wealth relations. James Madison understood this. In the Federalist, Madison spoke for the framers when he wrote, "Those who are creditors and those who are debtors, fall under a like discrimination. The first object of government is the protection of the diversity of the faculties of men, from which the rights of property originate."(5)

With American industrialism and land expansion in full swing following the Civil War, the rich found even more to cheer about in court decisions. In 1872, the Supreme Court ruled in the

Slaughterhouse case in Louisiana that monopoly did not violate constitutional or legal proscriptions. They deemed that "equity intervenes only to protect property rights." The precedent was firmly established that bigness in business was better and that corporations had special rights and privileges.

The "empire builders" who ran the corporations picked up the message. Men like Cornelius Vanderbilt in railroad and shipping, Andrew Carnegie in steel, Andrew Mellon in banking, and John D. Rockefeller in oil had few qualms about working the thin edge of legality between criminality and sound business in their relentless quest for power, profit and prestige. The brand of legalized capitalist plunder they brought to commerce and industry set the trend; Reagan and his merry band of modern day robber barons merely continued in their well-established tradition.(6)

Suite and Street Crime: Two Sides of the Same Coin

Before corporate criminals cross the legal line, they carefully weigh the risks and rewards, or what economists term the "opportunity cost", of crime. If they feel they can evade arrest, they will take the risk. They know the pay-off can be more wealth, power, and prestige among their peers in business and in government. They understand the rules of the game. They know that American society is a commodity culture. At its worst, it reduces individuals to objects of value to be used and discarded once their value is ended.

The quest for power demands a toughness, savvy, and manipulation to get maximum use out of those commodity objects. When corporate executives attain success, the media and general public applaud them as men and women of vision, confidence and self-esteem. Those who grease the wheels of capitalism are not born leaders. They are encouraged, notes educator James Comer, to develop their "rugged individualist" talents at an early age: "Indeed some white youngsters with undesirable characteristics—those of a bully, a manipulator, an exploiter—eventually do well in politics and business where such traits are all too often an asset."(7)

Is this profile of the future white collar crook or political power broker different from that of many young blacks? If suite criminals are adept at manipulating and intimidating people in their grab for wealth and power, can't the same be said for the young black who manipulates and intimidates to survive and advance? Corporate crime and street crime are inseparably bound. Illicit profit-seeking whether by the rich and powerful or the poor and powerless requires the victimization of others.

Since the rich and powerful set the value standards in America, they influence young blacks. If corruption exists at the top and the means justifies the end—wealth, power, and status—the implicit message is that society sanctions it. There is no right or wrong, morality or ethics; just don't get caught. Former U.S. Attorney General Ramsey Clark:

"Where white-collar crime is accepted, burglary, larceny and theft must be expected. If a poor man capable of a crime had custody of the company books he would rarely burglarize when he could embezzle. Nothing so vindicates the unlawful conduct of a poor man, as the belief that the rich are stealing from him through overpricing and sales of defective goods or that middle-class employees abscond with cash receipts."(8)

Although the young poor black lacks the same opportunity as the suite crook he reasons the same way. Before he burglarizes a house, steals a car or deals drugs, he carefully weighs the risks and rewards. If he succeeds, he expects his wealth, power, and prestige to grow among his peers on the street. This all makes sense to him.

He often displays the same keen talents of leadership, intelligence, resourcefulness, aggressiveness, managerial abilities, and verbal skills that corporate executives supposedly possess. Sociologist Louis Ferman, after conducting interviews with pimps, prostitutes, numbers runners, and drug dealers was struck by the "business-like attitude" they brought to their endeavors.

The 1971 "Manpower of the President" report noted that ghetto hustling was viewed by young blacks not as deviant behavior but as "a logical and rational option." The hustlers were drawn to the rackets by the possibility "of being on one's own." They wanted the same freedom and independence that the corporate executive has to control situations and make decisions.

A gang warlord boasted: "I make $40 or $50 a day selling marijuana. You want me to go down to the garment district and push a cart to take home $40 to $50 a week if I'm lucky." Even though the danger of arrest or violence is great, and the money to be made through street crime is often exaggerated, young blacks like him are more than willing to do whatever it takes "to get over." If they make money in their many hustles, selling dope, stealing cars, burglarizing homes, picking pockets or mugging old men and women, their status may rise among their peers on the street. Their peers may look up to them as symbols of those who're "making it."

This is why the young black must always present the right front (image) to the brothers and sisters on the street. His "threads" must be fashionable. His hair must be pressed, curled and styled. His assortment of gold chains, necklaces, bracelets, and rings must be visible. His "ride" must be the latest model.

To stay ahead of the police and his competitors, takes thought, planning and ingenuity. The same kind of ingenuity that successful corporate executives use to gain competitive advantage in the business world. Criminologist, Elliot Currie, after interviewing juvenile offenders in a predominantly black working class Berkeley community, noted the powerful pull that corporate power and consumerism have on ghetto youth:

"You can't build this casino economy that is based on stimulating greed, on making people think that the way you become a big person, a real person or a whole person is by buying stuff and having a lot of things and looking good, without expecting all this to be picked up by people down at the bottom of the social structure."(9)

There is no room for indecisiveness in the world of the competitive hustler. The successful dope dealer, gang leader, or strong arm robber must be confident, assertive, and shrewd. He is bending and twisting the coping skills that enabled blacks to survive slavery and decades of racial abuse for his own personal gain.

What many sociologists don't understand is that young blacks have a rich support system in the black community to draw on to boost their self-esteem. The most important are their peers and family. These individuals exert influence among African-Americans. They are strong and visible role models for the young.

Blaming the Victim

Although self-esteem has never been in short supply among young blacks, a generation of psychologists and sociologists insist that crime and social deviancy among young blacks results from poor self-image and low self-esteem.

How did they come to this erroneous view of blacks and why do they continue to perpetuate it? It sounds odd, but it's probably true to say that children's play dolls did blacks in. In 1949, black psychologists, Kenneth and Mamie Clark, conducted a series of tests to determine whether black children preferred to play with black or white dolls. When the majority of black children chose white dolls, the Clark's concluded that black children had poor self-identity and low self-esteem.

The Clarks had a noble aim. They wanted to show the emotional and social damage that racism and segregation had on young blacks. The NAACP used the results of the Clark tests to argue against school segregation before the Supreme Court during the early 1950s.

Meanwhile many psychologists distorted their findings. They blamed low educational performance, chronic welfarism, suicide, depression, ill health, and crime and violence among blacks on poor self-image and low self-esteem.(11)

This nonsense went unchallenged until the early 1970s, when black psychologists, suspicious of the earlier testing methods and conclusions, conducted their own tests. They charged that the doll tests were an invalid means of measuring self-esteem, personal identity, group preference, and racial awareness. They asked: Could it have been that the black children played with white dolls because there were no black dolls? To what extent were the children influenced by their peers who also did not have access to black dolls? Did their parents buy black dolls for them? If parents had more black dolls available during the 1940s and 1950s would they have bought them and encouraged their children to play with them?

This is not to say that the deep scars of racism and color-phobia have not left damaging marks on the psyches of many black children (and adults). Some African-Americans have regarded their "blackness" as a badge of shame and contempt. They have taken out their feelings of inner rage and self-deprecation on other blacks. But, as later studies confirmed, "self-hate" is a catch-all term that many researchers incorrectly use to blame all signs of racial pathology on blacks.

In several studies that tested racial attitudes among white and black kindergarten children at five predominantly black schools and two white suburban schools, the worst researchers found was that black children more frequently misidentified themselves than the whites. But the black children showed no preference for either race in their positive and negative role assignments. These studies were done in 1966 before the upsurge in the Black Pride and Black Power movements.

The tests that controlled for social and economic differences and interracial contacts among blacks, found that children from black working class homes preferred black dolls, while middle-class blacks showed preference for white dolls. They attributed the choice of black dolls among working class children to the greater support and exposure to the stable institutions within the black community.

Even when black children rejected black dolls, it did not mean that they disliked themselves or their color. They still possessed a good personal image, viewed their friends positively, and were capable of making productive choices and decisions. Other researchers noted that when black (and white) children received strong reinforcement of black social and cultural values from parents and their community, blacks overwhelmingly chose the black dolls.

There were even some white children who chose black dolls in the tests. No one, however, questioned their self-esteem. Earlier researchers also ignored the fact that in the Clark tests more than one-third of the black children rejected the white dolls as "being not like themselves."(12)

If much of white society believed that black children were socially defective, then why bother trying to educate them? Many white teachers proceeded on just that premise. In nearly every study done on teacher attitudes from the 1940s to the present, white educators have consistently described black children as "talkative," "lazy," "disruptive," "ignorant," "dangerous," and "deviant." The teachers brought their prejudices and stereotypes to the classroom. They did not teach and when their vicious self-fulfilling prophecy came to pass, they stepped back and smugly blamed black students for being intellectually inept.

An especially vicious by-product of racist teacher attitudes is the tracking system. Based on a 1986 National Science Foundation survey of 1,200 public and private schools and 6,000 teachers, the Rand Corporation found that black and Hispanic students are seven times more likely to be placed on a "low ability" track than white students. A low ability track almost always mean that these students will end up in non-college, vocational training courses that teach marginal or obsolescent skills. Rand could only conclude: "tracking fails to increase learning" and "widens the achievement gaps between students."

If black and Hispanic students are judged "low ability," it also should not be a surprise that the teachers assigned to teach them may not possess the most sterling educational credentials. The Rand study confirmed that 88 percent of math and science teachers in predominantly white schools were state certified. In predominantly black and Hispanic schools only 54 percent held state certifications.

That is not all. Studies have shown a direct link between low tracking and delinquency, irrespective of the sex or social class of the individual.

The students are not dumb. When they are put on a lower track they know exactly what the school system is telling them: "The children know when they are able to accomplish something and when they are failing." says Kenneth Clark, "They know when they are being relegated to the dung heap of academia. I don't know a single child who is so unintelligent as not to know when his school has given up on him." The problem has never been the low aspirations or low self-esteem of black students and parents, but the low aspirations and low self-esteem of their teachers.(13)

The worst part of this was that many educators knew better. As early as 1952, researchers noted that the classroom ability and career aspirations of black children equalled or exceeded those of whites. Tests conducted on groups of elementary and high school students in Baltimore in 1971 found that the black students scored consistently higher on measures of academic expectations, self-esteem, and career goals than white students.

Career aspirations and high self-esteem mean little if good jobs and economic opportunities are reserved for whites. And that is still the case. The Vera ethnographic study on youthful offenders found that whites dropped out of high school as frequently as did blacks but they were still able to find jobs through friends, family networks, and labor force contacts.(14)

When black youth cannot achieve their dreams, the consequences can be enormous. Bigger Thomas: "I wanted to be an aviator once. But they wouldn't let me go to the school where I was suppose' to learn it. They built a big school and then drew a line around it and said that nobody could go to it but those who lived within the line. That kept all the colored boys out." In Richard Wright's *Native Son*, Thomas acts out his rage and commits two heinous murders.

Like Bigger Thomas, Michael B. Green also had his dream: "I went almost all the way through high school. I got good grades, I was in the band—but I never got the attention I wanted, so I left and joined the gang." The 22 year-old Green is currently serving a sixty-three-month sentence in California for drug trafficking.(15)

Green's testimony also tells us why gangs have become a fixture in black communities. They are an extension of family and they enhance self-esteem by giving young blacks a sense of identity, peer group support, warmth, and personal validation. The gang becomes their surrogate father, mother, "Dutch Uncle," and Big Brother all rolled into one.

In good or bad times, gang members become their source of comfort and protection. When a gang member is killed, the other members usually turn out en masse to honor their fallen comrade. They often act as the pall bearers at the funeral and crowd around the gravesite to pay their final respects. As one gang member put it following the death of his "homeboy": "Norman was someone who died for his set."

This is why colored scarves, handkerchiefs, shirts, pants, and stylish designer sportswear have become so important to gang members. They cement gang allegiance and identity and serve as material symbols of the success and status that society denies. "They feel the system is closed off to them," notes sociologist Elijah Anderson, "And yet they're bombarded with the same cultural apparatus that the white middle-class is. So they value these 'emblems', these symbols of supposed success. Many young blacks are willing to die for and kill others for those 'emblems' and in defense of their set."(15)

With the spread of the drug trade in African-American communities during the Reagan-Bush era, youth gangs have become even bigger and more dangerous players. In some cities, black gangs now provide a hierarchical network for drug trafficking. To protect their profits from rivals and other hostile predators, gang members have compiled storehouses of automatic and semi-automatic weapons. How they get these guns is still pretty much a mystery. Are they bought, stolen, or being shipped into the ghetto from outside? Many blacks find it difficult to believe that teenagers, no matter how street-wise or capable, can get their hands on these kinds of sophisticated weapons without help from outside drug cartels or syndicates. If that is the case, then the high levels of violence are carefully designed to destabilize African-American communities in order to make drug dealing and use even more lucrative.

Because they are an intricate part of that violence, the Michael Greens' will continue to wreak havoc in African-American communities, and they will continue to land in prison. They want the status and identity of the gang and the riches of white society. And they are willing to pay the price.

Ticket Out Of The Ghetto?

Many young blacks like Green are astute enough to understand that they are deprived not because of their personality or intelligence but because of their color and class. The crimes they commit reflect both the greed of corporate America and a desperate need to break the stranglehold of poverty.

The young poor black intuitively realizes the eloquent truth of W.E.B. DuBois in *The Souls of Black Folks*, "To be a poor man is hard, but to be a poor race in a land of dollars is the very bottom of hardships." No matter how many hustles or games unemployed young blacks devise to "get over," few will escape their poverty. Their dilemma is not new. (16)

For nearly a century, black leaders have warned that racism and poverty spawn crime. The first Hampton Negro Conference held in 1898 attributed the increase in black crime as "due largely to industrial conditions as well as other evils." Resolutions at the Ninth Conference for the Study of Negro Problems at Atlanta University in 1904, directed by DuBois, passed resolutions that called for the end to Jim Crow and peonage laws: "The methods of punishment of Negro criminals is calculated to breed crime rather to stop it."(17)

Today white society still engages in wasteful delusions when it expects young, poor blacks to stay in school, get a job, and be productive-law-abiding citizens, when they see no future. University of Illinois criminologist Darnell Hawkins notes: "Telling kids to 'say no to crime' is absurd if they live in areas with no career opportunities." Thanks largely to the economic crisis of the

Reagan-Bush era, most young, poor blacks are trapped in these areas. The economic figures tell the sad tale of many young blacks, 16 to 24-years-old. Between 1980-1986, they suffered:

—An unemployment rate of 32 percent

—A family poverty rate of 50 percent

—A high school drop out rate of 33 percent

—A 25 percent decline in college enrollment.

—A non-labor participation rate of 34 percent (meaning they have ceased looking for work).

The average Black family income dropped from $17,595 in 1973 to $16,786 in 1987. The median income of full-time black workers fell ten percent from 1979 to 1987. Relative to whites, blacks fell further back. In 1970, the income per capita income gap was sixty-one percent by 1988 it had dipped to 57 percent. Overall, black families had $111 billion fewer dollars than white families. In 1989, the median net wealth of black families was $735.00 compared to $7,729 for white families.

By 1987, nearly one out of three blacks were officially classified as poor. The measurable drops in home ownership, health care, housing quality and availability, life expectancy, infant survival rates and college educational opportunities among blacks add to the bleak picture. There appears to be no end in sight. "We're creating a terrible mess out there," says Currie. "No mistake about it, the conditions are getting worse."(18) There is no mistake about it. Blacks are the prime casualties of the structural crisis of corporate capitalism. The OPEC price rises, foreign competition, inflationary pressures and the industrial shrinkage in the 1970s ushered in the era of economic belt-tightening. The technological transformation of American industry increased the demand for an educated and technically trained workforce.

The Reagan administration policies accelerated the process. The wave of plant closures, mergers, leveraged buy-outs and government supply-side economic give-aways to the rich during the 1980s resulted in the loss of two million well-paying industry manufacturing jobs . They were replaced by thirteen million low wage, service sector jobs. This left the black poor even more marginalized and unemployable.

Robert Greenstein, director of the Center on Budget and Policy Priorities, says: "For every person who is in the underclass, there are at least ten other people who are poor." For the poor, the Reagan-era budget cuts and attacks on social programs delivered the crushing blow to their economic hopes. Welfare or minimum wage labor became their only avenue to earn money legitimately. For thousands of others, crime became the more attractive option for survival.(19)

According to the FBI's annual Uniform Crime Reports, the number of property crimes rose slowly during the 1970s, mainly because there were still CETA jobs and skill training programs, as well as higher funding levels for education and social services. As the programs were slashed and joblessness soared under the Reagan administration, so did the arrest and imprisonment rate among the poor.

Harvey Brenner, a social researcher at Johns Hopkins University, has shown a direct correlation between unemployment and arrests. For every 1 percent rise in joblessness, Brenner calculates that: drug arrests increase 8.7 percent; larceny arrests increase 2.8 percent; burglary arrests increase 2.2 percent, robbery arrests increase 5.7 percent; and homicides increase 3.8 percent.

In 1980, 2,375 million blacks were arrested; in 1986 the number jumped to 2,789 million. In 1980, there were 150,249 blacks in federal and state prison; by 1985, there were 227,137. That same year there were nearly as many black women in American prisons as white women—11,429 to 10,793.

The arrest figures also serve as a stark reminder that when it comes to equal justice, the deck is stacked high against blacks. In 1985, more than seven million whites were arrested—more than three times greater the number of blacks arrested. Yet only 260, 000 whites actually wound up in prison. They were far more likely to receive probation, fines, community service, or referrals to treatment programs than blacks.(20)

The types of crimes blacks were arrested for further reflected their deepening poverty. Throughout the 1980s, black arrest rates for theft and robbery were so disproportionately great that some commentators derisively called robbery the "black crime." Many blacks arrested for robbery repeatedly said that they did not view thievery, especially from whites, as a crime, but rather taking goods denied them by society. Robbery, to them, was their desperate way of "getting even" with society for their shabby treatment.

Rape was another crime in which the black poor victimized each other. The higher the income the less likely that a black woman will be raped. The rape rate for black women with incomes above $10,000 was 22 per 100,000. By contrast, a black welfare mother or woman from a family whose income was below $7,500, the rate was 237 per 100,000 yearly.

Perhaps more than any other type of victimization, the danger of rape has heightened the fears of black women about travelling city streets after dark. In response, black women in Los Angeles, New York, and Washington, D.C. have organized "Take Back the Night" candle-light rallies and night demonstrations to protest the unsafe conditions.

As the economic plight of blacks steadily deteriorated, the prisons were filled with the poorest of the poor and the least educated blacks. A survey by the Law Enforcement Assistance Administration in 1974, found that 64% of black prisoners earned less than $6,000, 39 percent were unemployed, and less than half completed high school. A decade later, the income and education figures for black prisoners showed higher drop-out rates, unemployment, and lower family incomes. (21)

Poverty alone insured that many more African-Americans charged with misdemeanors would languish behind bars in city and county jails simply because they could not afford bail. A study of bail practices by New York City courts in 1965 revealed that 25 percent of all defendants could not make bail when it was as low as $500, 45 percent at $1,500, and 63 percent at $2,500. With rising costs and more stringent requirements for bail, even more blacks remain locked away pending trial or disposition of their cases. Capital punishment in reality means without capital you receive punishment. For these men and women convicted of no crime, jail remains a form of "preventive detention." The pressure on them to plead guilty and plea bargain a sentence is enormous.

Finally, even when black lawbreakers do evade imprisonment, the take from their thefts are hardly the stuff of criminal empire building. An estimated sample of the take from single crimes in Brooklyn in 1980 are fairly representative of what black youth can expect from their "labors." The average net value of a single larceny was $80.15, robbery, $134.09, burglary $451.81, and weekly marijuana sales $200. Hardly the stuff of criminal empire building.(22)

While racism, poverty and greed are the combustible elements that have propelled African-American communities into a dreadful circle of crime and violence, the media adds its own fuel. It daily tells young blacks how they should think and act, and whites how they should think and act toward them.

3

The Mugging of the Black Image

For the month of August, 1990, the author did an informal survey of all editions of the New York Times, L.A. Times, the Wall Street Journal, Time, and Newsweek. There were more than thirty-seven news items and features on crime and drugs. Blacks were well-represented in the coverage. They were pictured in handcuffs, being held at gunpoint, in court awaiting trial, in prison, on the street selling drugs, and as murder victims.

Even when the news story or feature does not deal with drugs, street crime or poverty, blacks are still fair game. Newsweek in one cover story, "The Mind of a Rapist," promised an impartial psychological probe of why men commit rape. Superimposed on the front was the face of a white male. Inside, Newsweek presented statistics that showed rape cut across all racial and ethnic lines. The figures strongly indicated that white females have a greater chance of being raped by a white male than a black female by a black male.

Yet four out of the five pictures in the story were of blacks. They showed a black policeman writing a report, a black suspect being arrested, two black women being trained in self-defense, and a profile of a young black accused of a campus rape. The four pictures were juxtaposed with the fifth shot of a white rape victim testifying before a congressional hearing. This gave the impression that white women were being raped by black men.

In a story on overcrowding of Philadelphia's jails, the New York Times showed a picture of Juvon Edwards a 24-year-old black who lived in North Philadelphia. The Times listed a long string of burglaries that Edwards had committed yet the courts released him because of lack of jail space.

Next to his picture was the picture of a white woman who had nabbed a purse snatcher in South Philadelphia. Her complaint was that criminals are being released. Why was her picture next to Edwards'? He was not the purse snatcher. Her assailant may have been white. We don't know and the Times does not tell us. All the public sees is another black criminal and a white victim.(1)

Using the material from the five publications I surveyed, I compiled a lexicon of the standard terms and phrases the media uses when the story is on "crime in the ghetto".

"crime-prone"
"war zone"
"gang infested"
"crack plagued"
"drug turfs"
"heroin addicted"
"violence scarred"
"chaos, anarchy, confusion"
"drug zombies"
"scum, leeches, losers"
"poverty syndrome"
"alienated and hopeless"
"ghetto outcasts"
"urban jungle"

The warning is clear. Crime, violence, and death lurk behind every doorway and under every archway in African-American neighborhoods. For their own health and safety, suburbanites best stay away. This is what these type of sensational press reports tell Americans about African-Americans and this is what they believe.

Crime gives the media another excuse to continue its century-old practice of manipulating images that promote a negative view of African-American life.

During the 1880s, respectable and staid newspapers and periodicals such as Popular Science Monthly, the Boston Daily Advertiser, the Philadelphia Evening Observer, and the Hartford Times, set the trend for vile and vicious stereotyping of blacks. In 1889, these publications heaped lavish praise on Phillip A. Bruce's The Plantation Negro as Freedman, which purportedly gave a "scientific" explanation as to why blacks were so crime-prone.

"Lasciviousness," Bruce assured, "has done more than all the other vices of the plantation negro united to degrade the character of their social life." Bruce juggled and doctored crime statistics to prove that emancipation caused blacks to slip into "intellectual reversion" and "moral decadence." The press agreed with Bruce that blacks would continue to menace white society unless severe controls were placed on them. (2)

With Jim Crow laws firmly in place in the North and South by the early 1900s, the media set out on a mission to protect white Americans from the "scourge of black crime." In historian Rayford Logan's survey of the press from 1901-1912, the New York Times, Chicago Tribune, Boston Evening Transcript, the San Francisco Examiner, Atlantic Monthly, and Harpers magnified and sensationalized black crime. Blacks were "brutes," "savages," "imbeciles," and "moral degenerates."

The media popularized the image of black men as rapists lusting after white women. President Theodore Roosevelt made it official when he lectured Congress during his annual address in 1906: "The greatest existing cause of lynching is the perpetration, especially by black men, of the hideous crime of rape." The Cincinnati Enquirer in 1911 went even further. Branding rape the "unspeakable crime, " the paper openly called for lynch justice, "The mob is the highest testimony to the civilization and enlightenment and moral character of the people."(3)

Black leaders battled back. They understood that the media's fabrications and distortions were designed to fan fear and hysteria among whites. Black educator, Kelly Miller in 1908 hit it squarely: "By fragments of fact and jugglery of argument he is made to appear a beast in human form whose vicious tendency constitutes a human plague."

Miller and other blacks were lone voices, many whites believed what they read and continued to depict blacks as brutes. In 1915, the film "Birth of a Nation," based on Thomas Dixon's popular novel, *The Klansman,* further convinced millions of whites that blacks were immoral savages whose only real purpose in life was to drink, gamble and rape white women.(4)

The News In Living Color

While few openly express this kind of crude racism today, the code words much of the media uses to describe black suspects come dangerously close. When a group of black and Hispanic youths in New York attacked a white female jogger in April 1989, many newspapers quickly resorted to name calling reminiscent of a century earlier. They labeled the attack "wilding," called the suspects "savages" and their action "animal like." The public believed that black youth were on the rampage looking for white victims.

When three teenage blacks were tried a year later, Newsweek used its cover to remind readers again of the "New York Grissly 'Jogger' Trial." The title of the inside cover story further drove the horror home, "Still shocking after a year." Newsweek used no such epithets several months earlier when Yusuf Hawkins, a black teenager, was murdered by a group of white youths in the largely Italian Bensonhurst section of New York. In general, the press ran sympathetic profiles of their neighborhood and gave the accused and their parents free rein to tell their story.

When the verdict was finally in and the three black youths were convicted of rape and acquitted on the charge of attempted murder, the Wall Street Journal was livid. The paper railed that these "criminals with adult-sized bodies and pure evil intent" would escape with light sentences. They demanded that New York and other states revamp their juvenile laws and start slapping youths with longer prison terms.(5)

The public is quick to pick up on this type of press coverage. They know that media terms like "savages," "crime-prone," or "crack addicted," do not apply to young white lawbreakers. As Boston Police deputy superintendent, James Woods observes, "The same thing that's happening in the inner city is happening everywhere. But because of the news media, nobody's looking at these other areas."

Since they aren't given the whole picture, many Americans feel that they no longer should regard civil rights and equal opportunity as priority items. In nearly every opinion poll taken since 1985, Americans list crime and drugs as their number one concerns. Public officials, quick to catch the drift of public sentiment, rush through more legislation mandating stiffer laws, police crackdowns, and lengthy prison sentences. Florida Republican Governor, Robert Martinez' boast, "I have now signed some 90 death warrants," sounds more appealing then to say, "I have now signed legislation that creates 90 new job and social service programs." Or "I have now provided funds for 90 new schools or hospitals." (6)

The way the establishment media reports street crime versus corporate crime creates the false impression that crime in America has a black face. Aside from sensationalized stories on organized crime czars, before 1985 the media rarely reported any wrongdoing by corporate executives.

The author's survey of Time and Newsweek from July 1980 through January 1985 uncovered exactly one story that specifically dealt with suite crime. There are reasons. Major corporations such as General Electric, Westinghouse, Mobil Oil, Sony, Warner Communications, Gulf-Western and Atlantic Richfield, either own outright, or are major stockholders in TV stations, radio networks, and the major dailies.

The days of the small, independent press are long past. In 1981, fifty corporate conglomerates controlled most of the business for the nation's television, magazines, newspapers, books, and motion pictures. By 1986, the number of controlling conglomerates had shrunk to twenty-nine. Before the end of the 1990s, the field will thin out even more. British publisher, Robert Maxwell predicts that "there will be only ten global corporations of communications."

The publishers, themselves, are wealthy individuals who share the same economic and social background as suite criminals. The press has a deep social and financial stake in maintaining the clean image of corporations and top business leaders. The smooth working of the corporate system hinges on public acceptance and approval of the financial practices, political methods, and personal lifestyles of corporate leaders and government officials.

No matter how much newspaper publishers and TV executives deny being influenced by "corporate sponsorship," the fact is, advertising pays the bills. McCann Erickson estimates that American companies spent nearly $100 billion on promotions and advertising in 1986. It costs an estimated $350,000 for two full page ads in the New York Times. With that kind of money on the line, few publishers will risk running hard hitting exposes' of the illegal operations of a corporation next to a costly full-page ad by the same company.(7)

The press can manipulate public opinion on black crime another way. By relying solely on data from the FBI's annual Uniform Crime Report, newspaper and TV reports can make the public believe that street crime threatens everyone, while suite crime threatens no one.

The Uniform Crime Report simply does not reflect the massive financial havoc corporate criminals, nearly all of whom are white males, reek on the general public. Arson is the only offense that could remotely be considered a white collar crime that turns up on the UCR's eight crime index. Government corruption and price fixing are listed as "frequently committed" crimes in the FBI's Part I offense section and they are not included in the UCR. Forgery, counterfeiting, fraud and embezzlement are listed in the Part II category reserved for "lesser offenses."

The FBI gathers its figures from local police departments. It makes no effort to independently verify their figures. The FBI correlates its crime and arrest figures to Census generated data which does not reflect regional population shifts. Also, because black males are persistently undercounted by the Census, the crime figures for blacks can't help but be inflated. No other federal agency exclusively publishes statistics on the number of federal crimes.(8)

The police also carry heavy weight in pressrooms. Crime beat reporters on nearly all metropolitan newspapers rely on police reports (and accounts) of crime incidents for their stories. Police departments understand this. They assume that ten tales of forgery and embezzlement do not play as well with reporters as one good account of a downtown street corner mugging or hold-up.

The media merges this grab-bag of crime misinformation with features on inner-city crime replete with pictures of black suspects. This batters the public with the image of blacks as the major perpetrators of street crime. The conditioning has worked well. One researcher having studied the Chicago Tribune's reports on crime and reader perceptions noted that the paper in several cases mentioned that the suspect was white, male and under 25. Still Tribune readers almost always identified the suspect as a black male under 25.(9)

The Media Double-Standard

America's one-dimensional view of crime might have stayed this way if not for the glaring scandals in business and government of the last decade. By 1985, the American public groaned under the huge weight of Wall Street swindles, HUD scandals, defense contractor abuses, and Saving and Loan frauds. The press could not ignore it. Soon the New York Times, Wall Street Journal, Time and Newsweek as well as major TV networks began to run more reports, news, and features on political and corporate criminality.

Yet increased coverage did not translate into moral outrage. The media still takes great care to let the public know that the crimes of businessmen and public officials are "alleged" or "purportedly committed." The public is continually reminded that these suspects are "presumed innocent." It makes sure that news accounts or feature reports on public officials or corporate chiefs under investigation contain full quotes and the accused are given ample opportunity to rebut the charges against them.

A case in point. On September 18, 1990 millionaire financier Charles Keating and three other defendants were charged by California prosecutors with 42 counts of securities fraud, and filing false securities statements . Thousands of elderly investors lost millions through the purchase of what they believed were government-guaranteed bonds from Keating's Lincoln Savings & Loan. The Los Angeles Times made only brief mention of the bond buyers.

The Times instead focused on Keating's personal plight. He was, "unshaven and looking tired," and "broke and in debt." There were extensive quotes from his defense attorney who swore that he was being illegally persecuted. The Times did manage to squeeze in a short comment from the Los Angeles District Attorney on Keating's bail of $5 million (Prosecutors initially planned to release Keating and the others on their own recognizance).

One could only wonder what the shape of the judicial system would be if poor blacks were accorded the same deferential media treatment? But then their total take amounts to a little less than the $200 million that Lincoln Savings & Loan investors lost in Keating's alleged swindle.

We may never know since the media produces no charts, or statistics on the nature, type and amount of suite crimes. The media seldom mentions the trauma and physical damage to the health and well-being of bilked investors. It does not broadcast angry editorials calling for more police, prisons, and tougher sentences. It does not promote fanciful theories of broken homes or malignant behavior to explain why Michael Milken, Ivan Boesky, or Michael Deaver commit crime.(10)

The media's chronic double-standard can better be understood by looking at the tale of two cases: West Virginia versus Marion Barry.

West Virginia has perhaps the most corrupt state government in America. State officials are so crime-prone that one newspaperman quipped that they would "take hemorrhoids if they were being given away." In 1988, the tangle of law breaking finally ensnared the state's popular multi-term governor, Arch Moore, the state treasurer, attorney general, two state representatives, the Senate majority leader, and two Senate presidents. During an eighteen month span, they were accused of bribe taking, perjury, embezzlement, influence peddling, fraud, and obstruction of justice.

While federal investigators patted themselves on the back for bringing indictments and winning some convictions, there were two problems. First, why had it taken so long to bring charges? The IRS had conducted investigations of West Virginia state officials since at least 1973. At that time, Moore was charged with tax evasion, but was not arrested. Once the scandal broke, the state attorney general and the state treasurer, despite allegations that they "misappropriated" millions of taxpayer dollars, were allowed to resign.

The state treasurer kept his $2,000 a month pension. Aside from scattered stories in local papers, the major media was silent. There were no probes or exposes on the "corruption in West Virginia." The exception was a front page story in the Los Angeles Times in July 1990. If not for the Times, the nation would have been unaware that an entire state government was on the take.

Even in the Times article, the reporters were gentle. They treated the story almost as if it was an amusing side show. They poked good-natured fun at the officials. Some examples: The governor ("he may have been dirty through and through, but he knew how to keep his fingernails clean"); the attorney General ("that handsome young attorney general with the catchy name, Charlie Brown"); the state treasurer ("a bow-legged 280 pounder with a nose big as a turnip bulb").

While readers were chuckling at the good-ole' boy cornpone style report, the looting of the state treasury was no joke to thousands of West Virginians whose average income was the second lowest in the nation. But then all of the West Virginia state officials were white.(11)

In neighboring Washington, D.C. it was a different story. Following an eight year probe, the FBI finally got its man. Washington, D.C. mayor Marion Barry was arrested and charged with possession of crack cocaine (later charges would include perjury). Newsweek's feature story, "Busting the Mayor," told a grim tale of intrigue, scandal, and corruption.

Poverty, drugs, the soaring murder rate, and government corruption in Washington, D.C. were laid on Barry's doorstep, "The sting shocks black voters and raises new questions about the capital's future." West Virginia state officials did not merit a similar cover story in Newsweek. If they had, it is doubtful that the magazine would have so cavalierly written off West Virginia's political future as it did Washington, D.C.'s.

Newsweek made passing mention that the initial charge against Barry was a misdemeanor. A charge, a Nation reporter called, "not equivalent to the moral equivalent of drunk driving." It saw no impropriety in the U.S. attorney's demand that Barry resign as a trade-off for dropping the charges. Rather it self-righteously assured its readers that Barry's arrest was not politically motivated, and that the arrest was not part of a racist plot to drive black public officials from office.

As proof, Newsweek cited the examples of white politicians John Tower, Jim Wright, Barney Frank, and five U.S. Senators under investigation for influence peddling in the case of a Savings and Loan executive, whose political careers were tarnished by scandals. What Newsweek failed to say was that none of these officials were arrested or jailed. NAACP executive director, Benjamin Hooks put it bluntly: "We have many white politicians who do a lot of things that might not be right and we don't see prosecutors going after them in the same degree."

That was not the end of the Barry saga. While the West Virginia story quickly disappeared from the headlines, the Barry case continued to play big on or near the front-pages for months. His sub-sequent conviction on the single charge of misdemeanor drug possession did not let Barry off the hook. The Los Angeles Times demanded that Barry be given the maximum sentence of one year in jail, and fined $100,000. Supposedly this would serve as a warning to politicians not to abuse their office and trifle with public morals. For some reason the Times did not accompany its expose of West Virginia corruption with an angry editorial calling for maximum sentences for all West Virginia officials. But then Marion Barry was black.(12)

Death Between Commercials

If the media can stage manage news and events to create the image of African-Americans as criminals, it can also turn them into victims too. Psychiatrist Roland Jefferson insists that black youth strongly identify with characters on the movie and TV screen. "The identification is so intense that acting out, more often than not, is the end result."

It is hard for young blacks to escape the all-pervasive reach of TV. Ninety five percent of American homes have a TV set. Sixty percent of the homes have two or more TV sets. In even the poorest black homes it is common to find two sometimes three TV sets blaring away in different rooms. The average American watches 20 to 30 hours of TV a week.

By the time a white youth reaches the age of 12, he or she will have witnessed more than 40,000 murders or attempted murders, and 250,000 violent acts. The Washington Post noted that TV crimes are likely to be "almost twelve times" more violent than real life crimes. Black youth see much more violence than this, because they spend nearly double the 25 to 35 hours the white teenager spends in front of the tube. (13)

There is no hard evidence yet that actual TV violence affects black and white youths differently. Yet the sheer mass of murders and acts of mayhem that black youth see on TV can certainly make them more willing than white youth to accept violent death as part of the natural order of things.

We do, however, know that TV plays a huge role in shaping the values and attitudes of black youth. It is more than just a socializer. In the absence of a parent who may work long hours away from home, TV has become a kind of "surrogate" parent for the young viewers. TV offers "content, moods, tones, and images that will interact with the child in such a way as to correct, refine and clarify his or her thoughts and feelings, just as a parent or another adult would do," contends psychiatrist Gordon L. Berry. Media experts such as Marshall McLuhan have repeatedly pointed out that TV clouds the line between reality and fantasy for youth.

For young blacks, the violence and criminality witnessed on the screen appears to carry society's stamp of social approval. TV provides them with negative reinforcement that violence is the accepted way adults solve problems and achieve gains. The panel report on the Causes and Prevention of Violence came to much the same conclusion regarding TV, "It can also be suggested that good triumphs over bad through violence—the main, as well as the only, course of action." Actress Marla Gibbs told a panel at the 1990 NAACP annual conference that "criminal behavior is being imitated by our children because it is being glorified on the screen."(14)

A study in 1982 by U.S. Surgeon General, Everett C. Koop, confirmed that youths exposed to excessive screen violence were more likely to commit violent acts in real life. Dr. William A. Belson studied more than 1,500 boys aged thirteen to sixteen. He found that the ones who watched the most TV were twice as likely to commit a violent act.

Why? Because TV cheapens life, and builds a cynical distrust in youth to social and human values. And even though most black youths, contrary to what the media suggests, do not go on wild killing rampages, it reinforces their belief that the world is a cruel, ugly jungle where only the strong survive. When young blacks kill each other, turning inner cities into what U.S. News & World Report calls "murder zones," the media must shoulder some of the blame. Young blacks are often acting out what they have likely seen many thousands of times on the screen.(15)

Children viewing 50,000 commercials annually desire designer tennis shoes and jackets and some will rob and kill for them.

While the media busily savages the black image through manipulation and the fantasy world of violence that young blacks daily play out in the streets of their neighborhoods, another tragedy is also being played out. This tragedy has torn families apart, destroyed lives, and done more to pit African-Americans against themselves than any other recent disaster. The tragedy is the doping of the ghetto.

There's as much cocaine in the Sears Tower or the Stock Exchange as there is in the black community.

4

The Doping of
The Ghetto

"The typical cocaine user is white, male, a high school graduate employed full time and living in a small metropolitan suburb. Bush administration Drug Czar William J. Bennett is certainly correct, but in the minds of white America the typical drug user is a black, male, high school drop-out, unemployed, and living in a large urban ghetto. (1)

Bennett's comment is instructive for another reason. It underscores the staggering dimension of America's drug crisis. Despite the carefully contrived impression given by the media that the drug crisis is a black crisis, it is an American crisis.

There are nearly 3 million cocaine users and 25 million marijuana users in America. The National Institute on Drug Abuse estimates that 40 percent of Americans over age 12 have tried drugs at least once. In 1988, Americans spent nearly $140 billion and consumed 70 percent of the world's illegal drugs.

As Bennett indicates, drug use by Americans cannot be categorized in neat racial terms. In a series of interviews with 372 white and black heroin addicts, researchers found that white males (93.4 percent) and females (80.5 percent) were more likely to sell drugs than black males and females (67.6 and 48.8 percent). On an average, white males and females started using heroin at an earlier age than blacks and continued to use it longer. This should not be too surprising. Whites who want to use or deal drugs generally have the advantage of less police restriction, more income, and greater accesibility to the drug market than poor blacks.(2)

The current American drug binge can only be understood against the backdrop of international politics and American society. The drug trade is a $500 billion world-wide business that involves syndicates, cartels, banks, corporations, government officials, law enforcement agencies and peasant growers. The CIA has been deeply implicated in promoting drug dealing among right-wing mercenaries and armies in Nicaragua, Thailand, Laos and Afghanistan.

The Reagan-Bush administration, for instance, provided the Afghan insurgents with weapons, supplies, and cash to the tune of $625 million, but looked the other way while the guerillas earned more cash through drug trafficking. Operating from their principal military base in Peshawar, Pakistan, the Afghans were responsible for 50 percent of the heroin shipped to the U.S. during the 1980s.

While the ghetto poor deal drugs to survive, the cash strapped, debt-ridden Third World governments are forced to produce and import drugs as a means to break their chronic poverty and underdevelopment. Under Reagan, Third World debt grew from $500 billion in 1980 to $800 billion in 1985. Export earnings plunged as falling oil, crop, and metal prices, along with rising interest rates triggered a massive capital flight from the Third World nations.

The drop in coffee prices had a particularly disastrous effect on the economy of Columbia. In 1988 coffee exports brought in only $1.6 billion in revenue while cocaine trafficking brought in $2.5 billion. In Bolivia, the poorest country in South America, cocaine brought in $500 million in revenue. Farmers in Peru, Bolivia and Columbia had little choice. Either starve or grow coca plants.(3)

The dirty business of drug production, import, and pricing takes place far from the borders of the black community. Anglo and Latin Drug magnates reap the vast rewards. White Americans enjoy their drug pleasures with little fear of arrest, while African-Americans bear the brunt of crime, disease, death, and prison that result from the lucrative trade.

The introduction of crack in the mid-1980s has caused even greater suffering. A mural on an Oakland grocery store labels a picture of Uncle Sam, "Uncle Crack" and shows him pushing a long line of naked and chained black slaves to a door marked suicide. This is not far-fetched when one considers that African-Americans are 50 percent of emergency room admissions for heroin addiction, 55 percent for cocaine addiction, and sixty percent for PCP use.

More than 25 percent of those treated for drugs in 1987 were blacks. Meanwhile, 25 to 30 percent of AIDS cases were black. Most of them contracted the disease through dirty needles or sexual relations with partners infected by dirty needles. In Washington, D.C. hospitals in 1988, an estimated 40 percent of the women having babies were drug addicts.

Many of their children will pay the price for life. By the mid-1990s more than 4 million crack babies will reach school age. They will show symptoms of mental retardation, poor cognitive skills, speech defects, hyperactivity, and a propensity to violence. They will require billions of dollars in special medical and educational services. Since most of them are black and poor, they will be stigmatized by a fearful society. "The school districts are scared to death, says Theadora Soyza who works with drug-exposed children at her Bronx Children's Learning Center, "you'd think they were getting monsters or something."(4)

More Media Myths

Much of the media has capitalized on the drug plague to create more myths about black crime. It plays on the violence to further color the image of black neighborhoods as drug-ridden zones of death. While one cannot minimize the sharp rise in homicides and health ills that stem from drugs, all black neighborhoods have not become killing zones where no one is safe. A New York research group revealed that 90 percent of cocaine-related homicides stemmed from busted drug deals, competition for markets and disputes over turf. The victims were almost always the dealers and users, not the general black population.(5)

The sensational accounts of vast fortunes being made by young poor blacks also makes good copy. So the media tantalizes the public with tales of crack traffickers heading sophisticated, cost effective Mafia-type operations. Supposedly they come complete with command and supply centers and a trained network of salesmen, guards, lookouts, runners that deliver a product with corporate like efficiency to their clients. Some reporters go further and insist that ghetto drug dealing has spawned vast, organized criminal networks that control all gambling, rackets, and prostitition in black neighborhoods.

According to the New York Times (Rose 10) 17-year-old Michael H. is one of the thousands of budding drug capitalists in African-American neighborhoods able to support his mother on his new found riches: "I gave her $200 a day. I used to open at 7:30. Went to school at 8. I'd get the workers, get the lookout, and tell my sister to take care of the place until I got home from school. I earned about $500 a day. By 10:30 at night, the shop was closed."

Even the black press has jumped on the bandwagon. Ebony Magazine, in a special report on the drug crisis, claimed that teen dope dealers in "entry level" positions were raking in thousands of dollars weekly. (6)

When it comes to drug profit, ghetto dealers like Michael H. are usually the last person on the rotten totem pole. A more accurate picture of the life of the black dealer was given in a 1988 Rand study of imprisoned drug dealers in Washington, D.C. The study found that the average income from street dealing was not $700 a day but more like $700 a month—if they were lucky to avoid arrest.

For every Michael, there are thousands of young black men like Derrick, a 25-year-old street dealer in Los Angeles who was convicted for possession and sale. Derrick, along with a friend and a lookout-companion, were busted attempting to peddle a $20 rock of cocaine to an undercover officer. After plea bargaining, the lookout received a three year sentence in state prison. Derrick, awaiting trial, will probably join him—-all over $20.

Derrick and his companion will have plenty of company. The same day Derrick was awaiting trial there were 26 other cases on the judge's calender. The public defender called 19 of them "chicken drug cases." These are small cases of sales or possession of drugs where the value was negligible.(7)

In a sense these defendants are fortunate that their cases are being handled in state court. If they had gone to federal court they might have shared the fate of 20-year-old Michael Winrow. In 1989, he received a mandatory life sentence in federal prison. Winrow was not a cartel or syndicate head. He received his stiff sentence for possession and sale of 5-1/2 grams of cocaine. Under the new federal sentencing guidelines conviction of as little as 5 grams of cocaine worth about $100 carries a mandatory minimum sentence of five years.

Winrow got the maximum which is life in prison. A Seattle public defender notes: "It's the black guys, the nickel and dimers selling a little bit of drugs to keep their habit going who are doing five years. The white kid who sells 400 grams is not getting a five-year minimum.When interviewed after the sentence, Winrow did not tell a story of big money or wealth, he simply said: "In the black neighborhood it's a struggle for survival."

Urban League director of social research, Douglas Glasgow spent several months in Watts interviewing young blacks. He could confirm Winrow's story that economic need rather than the promise of riches drove him to sell dope. From his talks with Watts youth, Glasgow concluded that the young dealers "could not gain access to the controlling positions or the big sums collected daily. The drug system would never be a major source of income."(8)

Cooling Out The Ghetto

With the massive amounts of drugs in African-Americans communities, many ask: Is this part of a conspiracy? Is the nation's drug war in reality a war on blacks? Moviegoers may remember the scene in the movie, The Godfather, where the ruling Mafia Dons in New York are sitting around a big conference table planning their markets for drugs. One blurts out "Let's sell it to the niggers.'"

This is not just the stuff of movies. Given the history of drug use — I include alcohol and tobacco use here too — among blacks, one can certainly make the case that African-American communities have been a prime target for drug marketeers. During the Civil War, black and white Union troops relied heavily on opiates for medicinal purposes and as standard pain killers. In rural areas of the South, blacks and whites commonly used laudanum (liquid opium) to relieve pain and depression.

The first real attempts by racists to link drugs with black crime came in the early 1900s. Newspapers fed white fears with bizarre stories of black "cocaine fiends", "cocaine criminals", and "cocaine sniffers", supposedly on the prowl for white victims. In 1910, Hamilton Wright, a State department official responsible for drug policy, put the government's official seal of approval on the scare stories when he testified: "Cocaine is often the direct incentive to the crime of rape by the Negroes of the South, and other sections of the country."

A study of patients at a Georgia State Sanitarium refuted Wright's findings. Only three of the more than 2,000 black patients suffered from narcotic addiction while there were 142 white cases. But facts didn't matter. In that era of overt anti-black hatred and violence, it didn't take much to convince most whites that "drug crazed blacks were moral degenerates and unfit for equality or political rights."(9)

Following World War I and the massive migrations from the South, thousands of poor blacks crowded Northern slums. The number of black drug users began to slowly rise. New York City clinics soon began treating more black drug addicts than whites.

From World War II to the early 1960s drug use in the black slums was confined largely to the poorest and most destitute street corner junkies. Harlem writer Claude Brown remembered those years: "if anyone had asked me around the latter part of 1957 what I thought had made the greatest impression on my generation in

Harlem, I would have said 'Drugs.' Just eight years earlier in 1949, this wouldn't have been true.The only notable exceptions aside from the black street poor were black musicians and entertainers including Charlie Parker and Billie Holiday who used heroin."(10)

Cocaine, an expensive designer drug was out of reach for the black poor. The only takers in Harlem, says Brown, were the pimps, whores, and hustlers on the street all night.And for most of them it was a frill that they would buy only if they had made a big score.

The first major jump in narcotics addiction in black neighborhoods followed the urban rebellions of the 1960s. The ease of entry and widespread availability of heroin gave rise to the first alarms by blacks that drugs were being used to control discontent and pacify the community.

Langston Hughes gave a vivid account of the seeming indifference of the police to street corner junkies in Harlem after the riots tore through the community in 1964: "In front of broken windows, overturned garbage cans and other evidence of minor vandalism, sat or stood the addicts like zombies. They leaned in a daze over undrunk coffee in the few cafes still open. Like robots they went through the motions of living in drug dreams on corners where policemen kept post-mortem."

The Black Muslims were more blunt. They called it "Whitey's Dope." Malcolm X said,"It is no accident that in the entire Western Hemisphere, the greatest localized concentration of addicts is in Harlem.The press and public officials dismissed the charges of men like Malcolm X as the paranoid ravings of black militants."(11)

Meanwhile, alcohol and tobacco have, in some respects, been even more damaging to the health and well-being of blacks. For decades the tobacco and alcohol industry have mounted expensive publicity and advertising campaigns in black newspapers, magazines, and radio stations. Phillip Morris enlisted the NAACP's Benjamin Hooks and other black celebrities in ads to push their theme that tobacco companies have First Amendment rights too. The industry's message to blacks is: pleasure, relaxation (and escape) can be yours by downing a glass of Scotch or taking a smoke.

It has worked. Blacks consistently have been the major consumers of alcohol and tobacco products with 38 percent of market. And they pay a stiff price. They suffer far greater incidences of heart attacks, strokes, and lung cancer than whites.

In the past, other than the Muslims, few black leaders were willing to charge drug dealers and the alcohol and tobacco industry with deliberately "poisoning" the black community. But the current crack epidemic has changed that. Now some black moderate leaders have wondered aloud whether there may be more behind the drug epidemic than meets the eye. They ask how can the U.S. government invade countries, launch telescopes into deepest space, control entire economies of nations, yet seem so helpless when it comes to stopping the drug flow across its own borders.

Black leaders as diverse as Louis Farrakhan, Reverend Calvin Butts and even NAACP executive director Benjamin Hooks agree that the government has done little to keep drugs out of the black community. Hooks charged that the "power structure turned its back on the drug crisis among blacks until it ended up in suburban high schools—then we got interested."(12)

The air remains thick with suspicion. However, the charges of conspiracy remain just that, charges that cannot be supported with hard evidence. The most that can be said is the history of drug peddling shows that people who feel trapped and victimized will grab any means to escape. Drugs are a quick, convenient and pleasurable way for them momentarily to escape the harsh realities of their lives.

Drug traffickers thrive on this and will eagerly sell their wares to whomever can pay. Is it any wonder then that many African-Americans bombarded daily by the megaggressions stemming from poverty and racism are among their best customers? This does not prove conspiracy only desperation.

War On Drugs Or Blacks?

Proof, however, is not needed to see that the war on drugs is being fought out on ghetto, not suburban, streets. African-Americans comprise about 12 percent of America's drug users. But law enforcement doesn't read the numbers, blacks are almost their exclusive target.

To fight the battle, they have unleashed a full arsenal of paramilitary weapons and tactics in the ghetto. They give hard-nosed names like Operation Invincible (Memphis), Operation Clean Sweep (Chicago), Operation Hammer (Los Angeles) to get their tough crackdowns. Special units Red Dog Squad (Atlanta) and TNT (New York) ferociously pursue drug traffickers in black areas.

When the streets are swept, the courts and jails take over. In 1989, the Central division of Los Angeles Superior court processed 17,000 drug cases, more than two-thirds of the defendants were black. The number of inmates in California prisons jumped from 25,000 in 1980 to 90,000 in 1989, more than one-third of them were young blacks. Throughout 1989 in Chicago, 120 persons each day were charged with possession or sale of drugs. Again, the majority were black.(13)

When the question is asked: Where are the white defendants? The police and prosecutors have a ready answer: "There's as much cocaine in the Sears Tower or the stock exchange as there is in the black community," says Charles Ramsey, head of the narcotics division of the Chicago Police Department, "but those guys are harder to catch." Those deals are done in office buildings, or in somebody's home. But the guy standing on the corner, he's almost got a sign on his back. These guys are just arrestable.

What about the majority of law abiding blacks who don't stand on street corners with a sign on their back saying "arrest me"? In nearly every major city, black professional and business persons have been stopped, frisked and their cars searched under the guise of looking for drugs.

During a month in 1989, Atlanta police targeted the city's public housing projects for their get tough policy on drug dealers. Cars were towed and impounded, residents were ticketed for minor traffic violations, and units were searched. More than 4,800 arrests were made. 3,700 were for traffic violations. Another 500 were for misdemeanor charges. Only a small number of those arrested were charged with drug dealing.(14)

Atlanta is hardly unique. The scene is repeated in nearly every city. HUD makes it even easier to harass residents of public housing in the drug search. Under 1988 HUD guidelines, police and federal agents can evict the relatives and family members of suspected drug dealers from housing projects without due process. The policy has been tested in Washington, D.C. and Chicago where a number of families were ordered by housing authority officials to move out.

With more than 100,000 persons on the waiting list for public housing and another 150,000 officially homeless in Chicago, the evictions could only make the city's housing crisis for the poor even worse. Neither HUD nor police officials have told the former tenants where they are supposed to go.(15)

As long as many Americans perceive the drug fight to be a "crusade in the ghetto", they are more than ready to throw even constitutional protections out the window. In a Washington Post-ABC Poll, 62 percent of Americans agreed to suspend constitutional freedoms if it would stop the drug traffic. They approve of student locker searches, random vehicle checks, and random drug testing.(16)

Many public officials lead the stampede to waive the 4th and 6th Amendment rights to counsel and speedy trial, and freedom from unreasonable search and seizure as long as they are applied in the black neighborhoods. They don't stop there. Special POW type camps for drug offenders, the death penalty for drug dealers, and arrest of mothers whose children are suspected of being born with cocaine addiction are also on the drawing board.

On paper it appears that the hard line measures will apply to rich and poor, black and white alike. In practice, it is quite different. Joe Morgan found that out the hard way. An all-star second baseman with the Cincinnati Reds and a recent inductee in the Baseball Hall of Fame, Morgan found himself being wrestled to the ground by two police officers at Los Angeles International Airport in March, 1988. The officers roughed up Morgan because he fit the "drug courier" profile, the Drug Enforcement Administration uses to identify suspected drug dealers. Morgan was released after the officers discovered their error. He later filed a civil rights suit against the city of Los Angeles and the officers.

City officials and the DEA denied that the drug profile targeted blacks for harassment. But it took a Supreme court ruling to clarify that the DEA could use the profile based on a person's behavior not on race. This did not quiet the critics who maintain that drug searches are used to harass blacks: "This happened to Joe Morgan," noted Morgan's attorney, Edwin Wilson Jr., "but it really is applicable to any black person."(17)

White Americans, spurred by the fear of drugs and black crime spreading from the ghetto to suburbia, are not the only ones willing to toss aside constitutional protections. Many blacks, desperate for solutions, unfortunately are prepared to do the same: "We know that perhaps in other circumstances these tactics and methods would be questionable at best, says black Texas Democrat, Craig Washington, But we're so tired of drugs that we relax our fundamental freedoms in the name of doing something about the problem.

The significant reforms the civil rights movement achieved in police methods and court practices are now fast becoming a distant memory. In the rush to clear their neighborhoods of the drug dealers, the issues of civil rights and economic reform are in danger of getting lost on the black agenda too. As an Atlanta police official put it: "They are going to continue to arrest the poor folks and say we're doing something with drugs. They're full of crap.(18)

This is precisely the point. Much of the drug war has been fought within the confines of black neighborhoods mainly because, as police officials admit, poor blacks are soft and accessible targets. With few funds or resources, small time dealers and users can be arrested and imprisoned in big numbers thus giving the police high scorecards for fighting crime.

Public officials reap dividends too. Since many Americans

have come to believe that the drug problem is mostly a black problem, officials can point to arrest figures to assure a nervous public that they are taking decisive action against the dope pushers. This strategy works because many Americans were conditioned by press sensationalism during the Reagan years to see the black poor as crime prone and dangerous. They are more than ready to blame them for much of the nation's social ills.

Still, the war on drugs was not always a war fought largely in African-American communities. During the 1960s, the war was fought against a different enemy. Buoyed by the civil rights and the Black Power movements, African-Americans had a cause to believe in. They were in the streets to battle injustice and oppression, not to deal dope or snatch purses. What happened?

5

The Collapse of the Movement

Who can forget the bright August day in 1963 when more than a quarter of a million people gathered in Washington, D.C. at the foot of the Lincoln Monument. The historic occasion was the "March for Jobs and Freedom," better known as the March on Washington. This was perhaps the civil rights movement's finest hour. The day when the conscience of the nation was stirred by the "I Have A Dream" speech of Dr. Martin Luther King, Jr.

While the eyes of the world were on the event at the Lincoln Monument, something else happened that day that few took notice of. A small item in the Washington Evening Star noted that the District of Columbia police reported only seven major crimes on the day and evening of the March. The same day, a week earlier, there were nineteen major crimes. A New York Times reporter who spent the day of the March in Harlem observed:

"Police cars patrolled Harlem's streets all day, thinking it would be a big day for robberies, with so many Negro residents away from home for the trip to Washington. But in the evening, the desk sergeant of the twenty-sixth precinct reported no robberies or other crime."(1)

Twenty-two years later a quarter of a million African-

Americans gathered again in Washington, D.C. for the first annual Black Family Reunion. They came to affirm in the words of National Council of Negro Women President Dorothy Height "the strength, resilience, adaptability, heritage, values, and coping skills" of blacks in America. The event was a joyous celebration of hope. Not one police incident was reported.

In June 1990, thousands of jubilant Harlemites turned out to greet African National Congress leader Nelson Mandela during his tour of the United States. Reporters were struck by the fact that arrests in Harlem and other black neighborhoods had dropped. The same week in Los Angeles thousands of blacks also turned out to cheer Mandela as he spoke at a giant rally at the Los Angeles Coliseum.

Shortly after the rally I spoke with an officer at the Southeast Division precinct station that patrols Watts. He gave me the arrest figures for May and June. Although they weren't broken out by week, I noted that there was a slight drop in the number of arrests for June even though the schools were out and there were more young blacks on the street. (2)

Coincidence? Hardly. The March on Washington, the Black Family Reunion, and the Mandela visit stirred pride and the feeling of identification and involvement with the liberation struggle in South Africa among African-Americans. The March, the Black Family Reunion, and Mandela symbolized hope for the future and the promise of social change. For that moment, social consciousness, group unity and racial pride replaced alienation, division and political impotence.

The Mass Movement As Crime Fighter

These events once more showed that social movements among African-Americans succeed only to the degree that they arouse the passions and consciousness of the middle-class and the poor. This is not unique to the African-American experience. In 1871, Parisian workers and slumdwellers took to the streets to overthrow dictatorship and battle for a socialist commune. During the struggle, ex-convicts and street criminals became the most fervent and dedicated revolutionists.

Frantz Fanon describes how the attitude and actions of the Algerian "fellah" changed during the war against French colonialism. "There are no more disputes and no longer any insignificant details which entail the death of a man. There are no longer explosive outbursts of rage because my wife's forehead or her left shoulder were seen by my neighbor. The national conflict seems to have canalised all anger, and nationalised all affective or emotional movements."

As Fanon says, the Algerian workers, peasants, and the urban poor had a common cause to fight for and foe they could attack. They no longer feared the consequences of French reprisals. Violence became in Fanon's words "a cleansing force." Not only did the crime and homicide rate decline among Algerians, but the incidence of suicide and other mental disorders also dropped.(3)

The spectacular growth of the Nation of Islam during the late 1950s and early 1960s was another example of how social movements transform victims of oppression. The Nation of Islam diligently followed the admonition of Elijah Muhammad "to go after the black man in the mud."(4)

Convicts, ex-convicts, hustlers and dope addicts embraced the Black Muslim doctrine of spiritual awareness, black pride, self-help, and economic control. The organization's rigid discipline and religious teachings gave them a strong sense of direction, hope and self-fulfillment.

The Muslim program was so effective in reducing drug addiction among its adherents that even some police officials grudgingly praised their work. No one in the organization better symbolized the powerful effect of black consciousness than "Detroit Red." The political and spiritual journey of "Detroit Red" to Malcolm X forever symbolizes the triumph and redemption of the human spirit. In his early years, Malcolm X was a pimp, hustler, and thief, and he served four years in state prison. Malcolm later told of the transformation that brought him to the Nation of Islam:

"You let this caged-up black man start thinking, as I did when

I first heard Elijah Muhammad's teachings: let him start thinking how, with better breaks when he was young and ambitious he might have been a lawyer, a doctor, a scientist, anything. That's why black prisoners become Muslims. The white man is the devil is a perfect echo of that black convict's lifelong experience."(5)

After his release, Malcolm became a Muslim minister. He took to the streets of Philadelphia, Washington, D.C. and New York delivering Muhammad's message to the brother "in the mud." They listened because Malcolm spoke their language and they could identify with his personal struggles to change his life. Hundreds joined, and by the early 1960s Muslim Mosques were operating in cities across the country. After his break with the Nation of Islam in 1964, Malcolm continued to grow in stature and influence, both as a leader and political strategist.

Like Malcolm, George Jackson made his mark as convict turned political leader. A small time robber, serving a life sentence in California's San Quentin prison, Jackson's letters from prison made him a cause celebre in the black movement in the late 1960s. Jackson described the change: "For the first four years in prison I studied nothing but economics and military ideas. I met black guerrillas, George 'Big Jake' Lewis and James Carr, W.L. Nolen, Bill Christmas, Tony Gibson, and many many others. We attempted to transform the black criminal mentality into a black revolutionary mentality."(6)

While radical political ideas changed the lives of Malcolm, Jackson, Eldridge Cleaver and other black prisoners, the civil rights movement had a similar liberating influence on ordinary blacks. In an experiment at a Southern black college in 1961, students were asked to volunteer for a mythical "Students for Freedom Movement." Researchers noted that the students most enthusiastic about involvement in direct action had higher confidence levels then the others. They concluded that these students "had clearly shaken off the effects of the traditional 'Negro' role."(7)

As the black poor became more involved in the civil rights movement that swept the South in the early 1960s, their lives also changed. During the Birmingham campaign in 1963, Dr. King was struck by the drop in crime in the city's black slums: "Mass marches transformed the common man into the star performer and engaged him in total commitment. Yet non-violent resistance caused no explosions of anger—it controlled anger—and released it under discipline for maximum effect."(8)

When King led marches against job and housing discrimination in Chicago in 1966, among his first stops were the bars and pool rooms. King understood that frustration and anger underlay much of black crime. His experience in Birmingham taught him that the hustler, the pimp, and the petty criminal could be enlisted in the struggle against oppression.

King was correct. Wherever civil rights activities were intense, crime dropped. To test the impact of marches on black crime rates, sociologists picked three Southern cities that had been the focus of prolonged black marches and demonstrations between 1961 and 1963. The cities were identified only as "town X," "city A," and "city Z" (From the description it was apparent that city Z was Birmingham). The researchers compared arrest rates during the months immediately before the civil rights demonstrations to those during the "civil rights months." In city Z, the number of assaults by blacks against other blacks dropped one-third during the "civil rights months."

When the civil rights marches ended the following year the number of arrests returned to the usual average. In town X and city A researchers noted a similar plunge in the number of blacks arrested for assault, robbery and homicide. A barroom patron told the researchers that "everyone in the bars and poolrooms " knew the details of actions and strongly identified with the marchers. In city A, gang members appointed themselves "guardians" of the civil rights meetings. At one meeting they were so enraged at the actions of the police that they pelted them with rocks and bottles.

The strong support the black poor gave to the demonstrations even surprised many civil rights leaders who had virtually written them off. One student leader in town X tells of one young black who was a chronic alcoholic: "He apparently was accustomed to being in the county jail, but while the movement was strong and active he never was in trouble, although he continued to drink." When the student later returned to the town, he learned that the man had been jailed again.(9)

The urban explosions in Watts, Detroit, Newark, and hundreds of other American cities also had a "cleansing effect" on the black poor. For the first time they controlled the streets in their neighborhoods. They ignored the police and took their revenge on the symbols of white exploitation. Their targets were the clothing, furniture and liquor stores that for years gouged them with high prices, shoddy products and poor service.

Looting to them was not a crime, but "whitey's payback." Tom Hayden, a radical activist in Newark during the 1967 uprising and now a California state assemblyman, vividly described the feeling of the crowds: "People who under ordinary circumstances respected law because they were forced to do so now felt free to act upon the law as they thought it should be. There were Negro gangsters and hi-jackers, on the scene too, but most of the people were taking only for themselves. One reason there was so little quarreling over 'who gets what' was that there was, for a change, enough for all."(10)

The fires cooled and the smoke cleared, but the black masses were in no mood to compromise their new found militancy. They had forced white America to finally pay attention to the ghetto. For young blacks the riots gave them hope that they could escape the fate that had trapped their parents in poverty. The change was exhilarating: "I don't do the things I used to do," one young rioter in Watts proudly boasted, "I used to split when the police came around: Now I'm proud; I don't run no more. I try to do something in the community; we're something today and respected."

Before the uprising, the young man had earned his keep through hustling and petty crime, now he and his friends were determined to do something positive in the Watts community. They formed the Sons of Watts organization. The Sons opened several businesses, a community center, and conducted clean-up and paint-up programs in the housing projects. They also established a Community Alert Patrol to stop crime and police abuse.

The Sons soon ran into problems. The police and public officials, plainly uncomfortable with the thought of blacks running community programs, threw up obstacles. They refused to grant building and use permits, turned down funding requests and harassed members. Frustrated, and angry over the interference, many of the Sons soon began to drift away. One by one the businesses closed and the patrol disbanded. By 1970, the Sons of Watts had ceased to exist.

A decade later, Douglas Glasgow tried to track down former Sons. He found that four were dead, several others were in prison, and others had returned to street hustling. Glasgow concluded that most of them "were back where they started from—an invisible part of the statistics of poverty, unemployment, and entrapment." With their hopes for community control and self-determination dashed, the Sons of Watts, like thousands of other blacks returned to the desolate reality of ghetto life.(11)

For a brief moment, some street-wise young blacks experienced a new political birth with the rise of the Black Panthers. Attracted by the tough talk and swagger of the Panther leaders, many young blacks flocked to the organization. But the Panther success was short-lived. Wracked by internal feuds and under intense government repression, the Panthers soon disintegrated.

Some observers who recall the period, wonder if they could succeed in organizing poor young blacks today. We can only speculate. But the best guess is probably not — for two reasons. The Panthers rode the crest of the political stirrings generated by the civil rights and Black Power movements. Black youth were more than ready to join any organization that promised to talk tough to "the Man." The same political mood simply doesn't exist at the present time. Secondly, the drug trade and gangs did not have the tight grip on poor young blacks then as they do today.

The Return To Normalcy

The Black Power and civil rights movements, which offered so much promise, had failed them. The death of King, and the growing white backlash during the Nixon years, had much to do with the failure of black leaders to develop tactics and strategies to address the needs of the black poor. But that was not the only reason. The systematic pattern of lawbreaking and civil liberties violations by the government also played a huge role in the movement's disarray.

As black militance grew in the late 1960s, African-Americans again found themselves on the receiving end of crime and violence, this time via the government. The FBI waged an intense, covert war on moderate and militant black leaders. Bluntly stated, the FBI's purpose was to disrupt," "misdirect," "discredit," and "neutralize" black protest. Malcolm X, King, black politicians, community leaders and numerous organizations from the Southern Christian Leadership Conference to the Black Panthers were all targets of the FBI's secret campaign.

The FBI employed a long laundry list of illegal tactics that included: wiretaps, mail intercepts, police spies and paid agents to deliberately plan and foment violence, planting phony documents, illegal police raids and mass arrests. The murder of Panther leaders Fred Hampton and Mark Clark in Chicago, and the trial and imprisonment of Bobby Seale were also linked to the FBI and local police intelligence agencies.

FBI officials also understood the impact that militant black leadership could have on black youth. They were determined to prevent that: "A final goal should be to prevent the long range growth of militant black nationalist organizations especially among youth." The FBI called for "specific tactics" to stop black groups from "converting" the youth. By "Black nationalist" the FBI meant any black group or individual involved in social protest.(12)

The combination of repression, co-optation, and disorganization by 1972, had effectively silenced the movement. Without a leader to rally the masses or a comprehensive program to address the mounting economic crisis of the black poor, civil rights organizations and black politicians largely confined their battles to creating affirmative action opportunities for the black middle class in business and the professions.

The new economic and social opportunities for the black middle-class proved a blessing and curse. Calling these opportunties a curse is not to belittle them, nor to blame the black middle-class for making progress. The gains came as a result of profound social protest and institutional change. The latter is especially important to understand because to some degree it explains why the poor were left behind.

Sociologist William Junius Wilson isolates four major factors during the 1950s and 1960s that contributed to the black middle-class advance: the sharp growth in government and corporate employment, expansion of managerial positions for college educated blacks, increased union involvement, and the continued migration of blacks from the farms of the rural South to the factories of the urban North.

The trouble was there was only room at the middle and higher rungs of the economic ladder for those blacks who were educated and technically trained to meet the changing demands of the marketplace. Lacking income, resources, and social connections, the poor were virtually excluded when the doors of the colleges swung open for African-Americans. During the 1980s, the economic fissures among blacks burst into gaping holes. In 1980, the black poor received 4.1 percent of black income. Six years later, the figure had dipped to 3.4 percent. Meanwhile, the top one-fifth of black families took in 47.4 percent of total black income. By 1988, an estimated one-tenth of blacks were affluent enough to move to the suburbs. And even though, the black middle-class did not completely sever their ties to their old ghetto neighborhoods, the income and skills drain did have a significant negative impact on those left behind.(13)

Their flight left the black poor leaderless and defenseless against the onslaught of attacks and abuses from an insensitive and hostile establishment. As the experience of the Sons of Watts showed, no longer were organizations able to channel the energies of the black poor into community-based campaigns for better housing, schools, jobs, business development and police abuse. By the mid-1970s, the issues which sparked the black activism of the 1960s, were relegated to parlor complaints or were left to a handful of disgruntled "movement holdovers."(14)

Established black organizations such as the Urban League and the NAACP began to develop an agenda which looked more and more like an agenda to move even more blacks into technical and professional corporate positions. Positions that the black poor could not dream of attaining. Worse, many of the new upwardly mobile black professionals and entrepreneurs, caught up in the go-go "Me first" and "look out for number one" frenzy of the Reagan years, had little time or inclination to trouble themselves with the plight of the black poor.

As the movement further distanced itself from the black poor, apathy, alienation and selfish individualism grew. The new generation of young blacks that had come along since the demise of the civil rights and Black Power movements were damaged the most.

Economically they were losing ground fast, even faster than black adults. In 1954, the unemployment rate for black teenagers was 16.5 percent versus 9.4 percent for black adults. Twenty years later, the unemployment rate for black teenagers had soared to a rate five times greater than black adults.(15)

The drop in income and jobs for black youth was only the beginning of their problems. The shifting social and economic priorities of black leaders stripped them of credible role models or support mechanisms to rely on. Faced with the prospect of being shoved completely out of the job market, a crumbling educational system, the constant threat of physical violence from gangs, and indiscriminate arrest by the police, the streets seemed to offer them the only hope for survival.

Watts and other urban ghettos became even poorer and more isolated. The social explosion of the ghettos during the 1960s now became the crime and violence implosion of the 1980s. The nation prepared to fight this new menace with an arsenal of judicial, prison and police weapons. Many Americans seemed ready to do anything to get safe streets even if it meant accepting their own myths and lies.

The victimization rate by whites of other whites for rape and murder (80%) is higher than the rate for blacks.

6

Myths and Lies

MYTH: *Since African-Americans suffer the most from violent crime it is in their best interest to support the death penalty.*

FACT: *In December 1989 in Boston, Mrs. Charles Stuart, a pregnant housewife, was brutally murdered and her husband was seriously wounded. The national press and the public were outraged. Massachusetts State Republican Party officials immediately called a press conference and demanded that the governor and the legislature enact a death penalty statue.*

What prompted the public frenzy? The Stuarts were the "Camelot couple" of white America, Young, and Yuppish. Their alleged assailant, William Bennett, was a black man from the Mission Hill District of Boston. The sole evidence against Bennett was the word of Stuart.

Shortly after the story broke, Stuart's version of the crime started to unravel. An alleged confession to a relative and Stuart's suicide appeared to confirm that Stuart actually killed his wife. Republican state officials, however, were strangely silent on the surprise turn. After all, if the death penalty they loudly demanded had been law, Bennett, if convicted, almost certainly would have gotten it. The state would have been guilty of killing the wrong man—a black man.(1)

And that is the problem. For decades, the death penalty has

become society's ultimate legal weapon against blacks accused of criminal acts. The figures tell the story. Between 1930 and 1986, more than half of all those executed have been African-Americans—1,784 whites, 2,083 blacks. For murder, the totals are nearly even—1,697 whites, 1,647 blacks. When the crime (or accusation) is rape, the death penalty is almost exclusively reserved for blacks. Of the 453 men executed for rape since 1930, 405 have been black.

Nearly all of them were executed in the South. They were arrested and convicted on the flimsiest evidence, usually no more than the word of a white woman. But what about black women, doesn't the death penalty protect them from rape too?

In Florida, between 1960 and 1964, the same percentage of white and black men received death sentences for rape. In almost every case the victims of the blacks receiving the death penalty were white women. At the same time, not one white man received the death penalty for raping a black woman.

One more fact. There is no record in any Southern state of a black man ever being executed for raping a black woman. Southern officials used the death penalty against black men not to deter crime, but to instill fear.

Largely because of the blatant racism in the use of the death penalty, the Supreme Court in 1972, ruled that the death penalty was cruel and unusual punishment and thus violated the Eighth Amendment. That didn't last long. In 1976, the court reversed itself and upheld the death penalty in three states. The door to the gas chamber swung wide open once more and blacks and the poor were slated to march in again in record numbers.(2)

The NAACP Legal Defense Fund in 1986 reported that more than 45 percent of those awaiting execution were black. Most were penniless, and unable to afford quality legal representation. After studying nearly 100 death penalty cases, the National Law Journal revealed that 1,000 trial lawyers assigned death penalty cases were disbared, suspended or had other disciplinary charges against them at a rate three times higher than other attorneys, and out of the 60 lawyers handling death penalty cases, half said it was their first case. The attorneys were paid minimum fees by the states, and their requests to hire investigators and other legal experts to present expert testimony were frequently denied.(3)

Charlie Young is an unfortunate example of the uncertain justice in a capital case. In 1976, Young stood trial for murder and robbery in Greene County, Georgia. The judge in the case announced that he would hold a night session to speed things along. New York Times editor Tom Wicker tells what happened next: "As the judge left the courthouse, he encountered Charlie Young's 72-year-old defense counsel, who said that he would not be present when the trial resumed that night. He did not ask the judge for a continuance. Instead, he left a young assistant, who had not been prepared in any way to handle the case, to cross-examine as best as he could six expert witnesses from the Georgia Crime Laboratory." Young, of course, was convicted and given the death penalty. His case was reversed on appeal.(4)

Aside from the obvious issues of racism, class bias, and unequal justice, the death penalty is a faulty tool to protect minority crime victims. Take Florida, which had the macabre distinction of being the nation's leading executioner in 1984. It executed eight and its homicide rate still jumped 5.1 percent. The two other leading execution states, Louisiana and Texas, have consistently had higher homicide rates than California and New York, where no executions have taken place.

The 14 states that do not execute had lower crime rates than the states that have the death penalty. Even more revealing, in four of the five non-death penalty states, the non-white population is higher percentagewise than the national average and the murder rate in each of those states is lower. With public alarm over crimes like the Stuart murder at a fever pitch, the pressure to enact death penalty statues in New York and Michigan with their large and growing population of blacks and Hispanics will remain intense.(5)

LIE: *Building more prisons will remove more criminals and make black neighborhoods safer.*

FACT: *Richard Nixon, hardly a bleeding heart on crime, in 1969 called the penal system "a convincing case of failure." Twenty years later it's even a bigger failure. The difference this time is that the flood of new inmates are black. If the trend continues, by the year 2,000, African-Americans will make-up more than half the prison population in America.*

In Florida, nearly one out of every two young blacks between the age of 18-34 will be in jail or under court supervision by 1994. Already, the total number of black men who have been imprisoned tops the 3 million mark, a number greater than the population of Chicago. America now locks up more blacks—230,000 in 1985—than openly racist and repressive South Africa. (6)

After studying data on the high rates of black imprisonment, criminologist William Nagel concluded that poverty and the unequal application of the law were the prime reasons for the swelling numbers of black prisoners. He also found:

—-No relationship between the crime rate or the amount of violent crime committed and the imprisonment rate.

—-No relationship between the proportion of blacks imprisoned and the rate of violent crime.

—-A direct relation between the imprisonment rate and the proportion of blacks jailed.

Nagel's findings suggest that prisons are designed more as society's quick fix method to control troublesome poor blacks than to punish the truly guilty. If that is true then prisons alone can only promote more false illusions of security. Indeed, Nagel was convinced that "the massive use of incarceration will not contribute significantly to the abatement of crime or to the correction of flaws in the social fabric."

Two British criminologists, Steven Box and Chris Hale, compared crime rates with economic cycles. They found that during periods of recession and high unemployment more people are sent to prisons than when the economy is stable. Box and Hale probably don't mean that bad times mean more bad people. Bad times, however, can mean tougher policing and a rash of new laws. When that happens the poor will be the first to feel the bite.(7)

A look at the types of crimes and individuals that are locked up confirms this. First the youth. Eighty percent of the prisoners in Georgia's four juvenile detention centers in June 1990 were black. All of the 110 youths serving time for drug offenses were black. Are these really dangerous prisoners who should be isolated from society?

Researchers at the University of Michigan's Center for the Study of Youth Policy said only half might fit that label. The others were there for minor drug offense and property crimes and could have been released into community rehabilitation or treatment programs. "What should be apparent to everybody," said Richard McDevitt of the Georgia Alliance for Children, "is that in our juvenile prisons we have more prisoners than criminals."

Maybe. But prison officials don't see it that way. In 1989, 41.8 percent of those in state prisons had committed violent crimes; 28 percent were there for burglary; 6 percent for car theft; 25.6 percent for possession or sale of drugs; and 4.5 percent for parole violation or drunk driving. A study by the California state legislative analyst revealed that 76 percent of prisoners in the state had a history of drug or alcohol abuse.

Despite the high incidence of substance abuse, the State Department of Corrections still spent $500 million or one-quarter of its 1989-1990 budget on punitive incarceration of drug offenders. At the same time, the state spent a paltry $1.5 million on drug treatment programs. The federal government spends 75 percent of its budget on law enforcement, not treatment and education.

While no one can say for sure how many of these individuals would be behind bars if help were available, it's certain that many of them would seek help. But help is not there and that frustrates even many police officials: "If even a quarter of the addicts walked into the courthouse today and said 'I give up,' there's no place for them to go," says an Atlanta narcotics official. 'The problem is that for years every one has viewed this as a law enforcement problem."(8)

As long as the color of those behind the bars is increasingly blacker, the public will continue to have the same myopic view. Prisons are society's answer to crime and they will continue to fail. Penologists estimate that 35 to 40 percent of offenders after being released will commit crimes. And once more they will be warehoused in a state prison. They will become even more bitter over there isolation from society. Rehabilitation requires tutoring, job training, and exposure to cultural and spiritual values.

With the current trend toward building hi-tech, computer-controlled prisons in distant rural areas, the likelihood is that black prisoners will feel more isolated than ever from their families, relatives and social supports. This can only reinforce their bitterness at being treated like societal outcasts.

Prison will continue to impose a special burden for blacks. A character in Claude Brown's Manchild in the Promised Land graphically warns:

"In jail, everybody's doing time."

"Yeah, man, but everybody isn't doing the same kind of time. There's white time in jail, and there's nigger time in jail. And the worst kind of time you can do is nigger time. (9)

Black neighborhoods will hardly be safer from men and women like these.

MYTH: *Tougher laws will protect African-Americans too.*

FACT: *In 1989, Michael Kelson, a 22-year-old black man, was arrested in Wilmington, Delaware and charged with the possession of 5.18 grams of cocaine. A resident of one of Wilmington's poorest neighborhoods, Kelson worked at odd jobs and did a little street hustling to "make it." After his arrest, a private attorney agreed to defend him for a fee of $1,000. Kelson's response, "Where am I going to get that kind of money?" He stayed in jail.*

Kelson was subsequently convicted and sent to prison for three years. He left behind two children by different women who will probably subsist on welfare at taxpayers expense. But Delaware state legislators were not thinking of young blacks like Kelson in 1988 when they passed a mandatory three-year sentence for possession of more than 5 grams of cocaine. They were thinking of their constituents in the suburbs who demanded to be protected from men like Kelson.

Delaware is not alone. Other states in the rush to quiet public fears over men like Kelson, passed tough new laws that required heavy fines and longer jail sentences for drug possession. In Indiana, judges can sentence a defendant for 20-50 years for possession of as little as 3 grams of cocaine. In Georgia, possession of small amounts of cocaine can bring a 20 year sentence. (10)

The idea, of course, is to remove the criminals from the streets. But what happens when they return? When released, Kelson will only be twenty-five and will have no skills, little education and no career opportunities. Worse, he will carry the indelible imprint of the ex-con. And no matter how many times Americans say that ex-prisoners "paid their dues and now deserve another chance," most will never get it.

When one hundred employers at Catskill resort hotels were asked whether they would hire a parolee, only one said yes. The interviewers purposely did not specify the race of the defendant. There was a bigger surprise. Interviewers asked 25 employers whether they would hire a person who had been tried, found innocent and had a letter from the trial judge vouching for the defendant's innocence. Only three said they would hire the individual. The conclusion: the presumption of innocence is only a hollow phrase in civic's book.

In the minds of most Americans if someone is arrested he or she must be guilty of something, so better play it safe and not have them around. For young blacks, the stigma of arrest almost guarantees that they will return to the streets to commit more crimes. The endless cycle of crime, arrest, imprisonment and more crime will remain unbroken. (11)

. As the Kelson case shows, Americans can rant about weak laws and soft judges, but the reality is that street criminals are locked up and prosecuted to the increasingly widening limits of the law. This has been true long before the present get tough climate. Charles Silberman in his Criminal Violence, Criminal Justice, found a close relation between arrests and punitive action.

For the 2,780,000 crimes the FBI reported in 1965, there were 727,000 actual arrests. Of these, 63,000 offenders served prison terms. An 8.6 percent punishment rate. On the surface this does appear that the legal net is loose and that many criminals slip through.

Silberman, however, looked closer and found that 260,000 were juveniles and their cases were disposed of in juvenile courts. As for the 467,000 adult cases, charges were dropped against 127,000. 162,000 persons pled guilty and their crimes were reduced to misdemeanors. The remaining 177,000 adults were charged with felonies. 130,000 of them pled guilty; and 30,000 were convicted in court. This means that 69 percent of those actually arrested and 95 percent of those prosecuted received some type of punishment.(12)

With the wave of mandatory sentences and get tough laws in the 1980s, there is little chance that convicted felons will evade punishment. For the Charles Kelsons there are few leaks in the justice system.

LIE: *More police in black neighborhoods will stop crime.*

FACT: *In 1972, the Police Foundation conducted a one-year experiment with the Kansas City police department. The intent was to measure whether more police in an area actually reduced crime. A commercial-residential section of Kansas City with a balanced income and racial mix was divided into three sectors. The sectors were labelled: reactive (no preventive patrolling); proactive (saturated preventive patrolling) and controlled (no change). They studied arrest rates for burglary, auto theft, robbery, rape, homicide, and the resident's attitudes toward police response and security.*

The Foundation discovered that tripling the patrols did not reduce crime in the proactive sector. Crime did not increase in the reactive sector, and the crime rate did not rise in areas outside the city. There were no significant differences in the number of crimes reported, arrests made or security measures residents took in either of the areas. In the preface to the Police Foundation's summary report, then Kansas City police chief, Joseph McNamara stated, "Routine preventive patrol in marked cars has little value in preventing crime or making citizens feel safe."(13)

Police visibility and high arrest figures are poor criteria to judge the effectiveness of law enforcement. Los Angeles police were conducting highly publicized massive "gang" sweeps in black neighborhoods in 1989, and arrested hundreds of young blacks on various charges from curfew violations to traffic warrants. Several shootings occurred within hours of the police action.

In black and poor neighborhoods police saturation tends to skew the arrest figures upward even when there are relatively few crimes being committed. If a crime is committed the standard practice is to round up large numbers of young blacks and hold them on suspicion. Most are later released with no actual charges being filed. A study of the arrest figures reported in the FBI's Uniform Crime Report in 1969 found that 28 percent of the 5.5 million arrests were of blacks. Forty-five percent of them were detained on suspicion and were released. A Chicago police official was direct, "Where you have more police you're going to have more arrests."

The police method of arrest, detention and release came under fire in Oakland in 1984 when six black policemen sued the city. The officers said they were harassed by their superiors after they objected to arrest quotas enforced in black areas. The U.S. Equal Opportunity Commission upheld the officers and ruled that the city was guilty of discrimination.(14)

Not only do more police in black neighborhoods not cut down the violence, but in far too many cases they have been the cause of it. Over the years, no issue has caused more black resentment than police shootings. Police killings in nearly every major city have sparked angry confrontations, mass marches, countless investigations, and lawsuits. Most of the blacks killed during the uprisings in Detroit, Watts and Newark died from police bullets. In nearly all cases, the victims were not snipers but residents either caught in police crossfire or unarmed looters. Militant black organizations, particularly the Black Muslims and the Black Panthers, have been special targets of police violence.

The percentage of blacks killed by police bear out the charge by sociologist Paul Takagi that "police have one trigger for whites and another for blacks." Chicago, 75 percent; Oakland, 79 percent; New York City, 60 percent; Atlanta, 76 percent; Newark, 78 percent; Birmingham, 79 percent; and Los Angeles, 55 percent. These figures were compiled during the early 1970s when the proportion of blacks in the population of these cities were much lower than at present.(15)

Blacks should be more concerned about the number of residents and organizations that are willing to get involved in the crime fight, than the number of police on their streets. Despite, the deployment of dozens of additional officers on the streets of South Central Los Angeles, gang violence, drug sales and other crimes continued to escalate in 1989. Finally, the community decided to do something about it.

In 1990, in Los Angeles, a coalition of groups, including the Nation of Islam, SCLC, the Brotherhood Crusade, aided by large numbers of community volunteers, organized the Taking Our Community Back Campaign. They conducted marches, held community fairs and instructed residents in crime prevention techniques. In the three-month period between January 1 and March 31, 1990 crime dropped more than 36 percent. Gang related murders dropped more than 45 percent.

The Campaign was effective because residents and organization leaders understood the economic and social cause of crime. The experience of a campaign volunteer is instructive: "Gangs pulled the license plates off my car, let air out of my tires. They would drive by my house throwing gang signs."The volunteer and twenty other members confronted the gang members, but did not threaten violence. Instead they offered to assist the gang members to enroll in school and find jobs. "They backed off," said the volunteer.(16)

Blacks, however, must be cautious about outside groups who come into their communities to fight crime. They can do as much harm as good. The Guardian Angels, for instance, gained glowing press coverage in the mid-1980s for their subway and street patrols in New York City. During the same period they attempted to set up a chapter in Los Angeles to "protect the community."

Their leaders, however, soon became embroiled in physical confrontations with local youths. The Angels contended that the youths were gang members. The youths accused the Angels of harassment. Whatever the case, the damage was done and the Angels found themselves virtualy isolated from the community. They had no measurable impact on crime rates.

MYTH: *When blacks victimize other blacks the legal system is there to help.*

FACT: *At first glance there does appear to be some truth to this. Many advocates of tougher laws and harsher sentences correctly point out that blacks are the main victims of black crime. Community leaders outraged over black street crime want the criminals off the streets and behind bars. There is no disagreement on this. The problem is how the laws are enforced and what are their consequences?*

As already shown, "black-on-black crime" is a media distortion. To the extent that blacks victimize blacks, they do it for the same reasons that Hispanics victimize Hispanics and whites victimize whites. They are close and accessible targets. In fact the victimization rates by whites of other whites for rape and murder —80 percent— is higher than the rate for blacks.(17)

When social and economic variables are considered, studies show that blacks are even less likely to victimize other blacks. A black accountant is less likely to cheat his clients than is a white accountant who has full power over business books.

The notion that African-American communities are better protected when black lawbreakers are severely punished ignores judicial reality. The harshest sentences blacks receive are for crimes against whites, not other blacks. A half century ago a Southern police captain was blunt: "In this town there are three classes of homicide. If a nigger kills a white man that's murder. If a white man kills a nigger, that's justifiable homicide. If a nigger kills a nigger, that's one less nigger." This devaluation of black life by racism has had horrible repercussions. It encourages disrespect for the law and greater violence among African-Americans. (18) Not much has changed today. The race, social and economic status of the victim rather than the crime still plays the crucial role in what punishment a criminal receives. From 1979 to 1983, nearly all of the black women who committed murder in Chicago and Houston were charged with first degree murder. Only 28 percent were sent to prison. The rest either received probation or had charges dismissed. In Dallas County, Texas in 1988, blacks served considerably less prison time for rape, robbery and murder when their victim was black.

Numerous studies have shown that when a black man kills a white the chances are great that he will receive the death penalty. The victims of all but 44 of the blacks executed in the South from 1930 through 1984 were white. Based on ten years of studies of black-white homicide patterns, criminologist Darnell Hawkins has established his own rating system for severity of punishment:

Most Serious Offense:
    Black kills white, in authority
    Black kills white, stranger
    White kills white, in authority
    Black kills white, intimate, family member
    White kills white, stranger
    White kills white, friend, acquaintance
    White kills white, intimate, family
    Black kills black, stranger
    Black kills black, friend, acquaintance
    Black kills black, intimate, family
    White kills black, stranger

Least serious:
    White kills black, stranger
    White kills black, friend, acquaintance
    White kills black, intimate, family(19)

Can anyone seriously believe that if William Bennett in Boston had been accused of killing a pregnant black woman and wounding her husband, Republican state officials in Massachusetts would have screamed for a death penalty law?

If blacks are less likely to serve lengthy sentences for crimes against other blacks, then it follows that the laws are not truly designed to punish "black-on-black crime." It is not unusual to see blacks released on their own recognizance or minimal bail for burglary or even robbery when the victim is black.

In most cases when the victim is black, the black offender will plea bargain a reduced sentence. The time the assailant may actually spend in jail will be far less than if the victim were white. When he is released, he will probably commit more crimes and his victims will again be black. And since police rarely return stolen property and state courts seldom provide for restitution or compensation for the victim, they lose on that ground as well.(20)

The sweep-the-streets policy can take a dangerous turn that the hard-liners may not see. Far from keeping one less victim out of the clutches of a criminal, the evidence is strong that more severe punishment without programs for support and rehabilitation assures that the offender when released will not only commit more crimes, but that the crimes will be more serious and violent.

Given the history of law and racism in America, blacks should be cautious of public officials who espouse the "slug the thugs line." Often the thugs they have in mind can become any black person who police deem is in the wrong neighborhood, wearing the wrong clothes, or driving the wrong car.

The police net as, Andrew Hacker surmises, can indeed be very broad: "Black muggers and murderers seldom dress in rags. Most of them are quite indistinguishable from black Columbia students and Chase Manhattan trainees, so that those subject to fairly frequent friskings would include people like Percy Sutton and Nigerian United Nations delegates, along with black ministers, shoe shiners, schoolteachers and writers."(21)

Caught between police inaction, and high crime, some blacks

are tempted to arm themselves and resort to vigilantism to protect their neighborhoods. This would do more harm than good. The prospect of African-Americans turning their communities into Dodge City free fire zones heightens the possibility that innocent people, friends and relatives would become victims. The hard core criminals would still go unscathed.

The Bernhard Goetz case proves that whenever citizens take the law into their own hands trouble results. In the celebrated case in 1985, Goetz claimed that he feared that the four black youths he shot on a New York subway were going to attack him. The public's glee was short-lived when testimony showed that Goetz' motives were less than heroic. A Grand Jury concluded that he had not acted in self-defense, and that the shooting was premeditated. Goetz was tried for attempted murder but in the racially charged climate of New York, Goetz was convicted and sentenced on a minor handguns violation charge.

In Los Angeles, Chicago and Brooklyn young black or Hispanic men have been killed by armed citizens who claimed they shot them because they thought they were going to rob or assault them. In several cases no weapons were found on the young men and there were no witnesseses to corroborate their story.(22)

If vigilantism, more prisons, more police, the death penalty, and repressive laws will not make the streets of African-American communities safer, what will? As I will show, there are far better alternatives for African-Americans.

An education task force must focus specifically on young black males.

7

SOLUTIONS

For many African-Americans, crime is the Trojan Horse that threatens them from within their communities. Every robbery makes them more fearful for their family and friends. Every dope bust makes them more fearful of their neighbors. Every murder makes them more fearful of other African-Americans. They are ready to take back their community, but African-Americans can only do that by fighting crime AND its causes.

This will take more than pious words. It will take honesty. African-Americans—indeed all Americans—must realize that bad genes, broken homes and the "criminal mind" do not explain crime. More police, prisons, tough laws and capital punishment will not end crime. Nor will money or social programs alone solve the problem.

Crime in America is a structural problem deeply rooted in the country's cultural, social and economic development. Theft and violence are committed just as easily with a pen as with a gun. Criminals do not populate the urban ghettos exclusively, they are also found in the penthouses and boardrooms of America. But that kind of crime does not seem to worry many Americans, black crime does. So in the search for solutions, Americans can start by observing some trends.

Crimes of property and violence reached their lowest levels

among the black poor in the mid-1960s. The reason: Black youth were organized and mobilized to fight for social change. The civil rights and Black Power movements gave them pride and respect. The urban rebellions gave them the feeling that they could control the destiny of their lives and their community. They believed that they could bring a hostile power structure to its knees.

But during the Watergate and post-Vietnam era that changed. Lawbreaking and the arrogance of power by business and government officials made Americans—black and white—cynical about their political leaders and American values. The civil rights movement, showing signs of disorganization, could not provide effective leadership for blacks. As more Americans began to question their country's values and institutions, and retreat into their own personal isolation, the needs of the black poor were forgotten.

The Reagan-induced poverty and unemployment of the 1980s brought more devastation to America's black underclass. Cutbacks in job programs, social services, the rollback in civil rights gains, a decline in high paying jobs in manufacturing requiring minimal education and an increase in low paying service sector positions requiring additional education, and the mounting rightist counter-attack further disrupted and divided African-American families.

Young blacks were now pushed to the outer fringes by an increasingly greedy and corrupt society. With each passing year, their TV screens were filled with startling events that made them feel even more like social outcasts, and reinforced their belief that society had one standard of justice for the rich and another for the poor.

They saw drug and crime kingpins raking in millions and living princely life styles while evading prosecution. They saw elected officials jailed or fined for accepting bribes or violating rules of ethics. They saw defense contractors, bank, S&L officials, Wall Street stockbrokers and government officials indicted for influence peddling, stock swindles, padding government contracts and real estate scams.

They saw TV hucksters bombarding the public with dozens of

flashy advertisements extolling the good life and commodity culture. They learned that everything is for sale, but it takes money, and where is one to get it? Greed and need drove them to crime, the only path they could take to attain the riches that corporate culture feverishly promotes as the American Dream.

The task during the 1990s is to renew the spirit, organization and dedication to social causes that motivated blacks during the mid-1960s. This is the key to bringing peace and security back to African-American communities. The barrier of isolation and alienation that young blacks feel must be broken down. This will require politically conscious leaders and organizations to sharpen the issues and develop programs to attain economic, political and social empowerment.

This is the long view. Until that happens, there are five immediate steps that African-Americans can take to reduce the danger in their streets.

Community Protection Councils

History shows that African-Americans have a long tradition of organizing to fight crime, delinquency and substance abuse in their communities. Before World War I, blacks formed temperance organizations, improvement associations and citizens leagues in Harlem, Chicago, New Orleans and Atlanta to pressure city officials to close bars, houses of prostitution and gambling dens. They mounted education campaigns designed to promote self-help, education, temperance, social and trade skills.

One of the most successful early efforts was the Colored Law and Order League in Baltimore in 1909. Outraged over the rash of robberies and murders in the black community, the League demanded that the city take action to revoke the liquor licenses of bars it identified as trouble spots. (The majority of them were owned by whites).

White public officials, accustomed to viewing black crime as the result of "Negro idleness and immorality," tried to turn a deaf ear to the League's complaints. But the League was persistent . It continued to protest and eventually forced the state liquor commission to revoke the licenses of more than 11 taverns.(1)

There have been many modern-day successors to the Colored Law and Order League. During the 1960s, black militant organizations mounted their own campaigns against crime. They recognized that black criminals were not modern-day Robin Hoods taking from the rich and giving to the poor. They were disruptive to community life and an obstacle to black unity. The slogan of the Community Alert Patrol, a black group that patrolled Watts after the 1965 uprising, captured the militant sentiment: "We support brotherhood, not the brother who's a hood."

The Panthers called on blacks to repudiate the "illegitimate capitalists"— pimps, dope dealers, hustlers and thieves—that preyed upon the black poor. Student Nonviolent Coordinating Committee leader H. Rap Brown tried to organize a group in New York to rid the community of dope dealers. Maulana Karenga's US organization in Los Angeles, conducted classes in African history, culture, and self-defense that pulled many youths from gangs.(2)

Today, in dozens of communities nation-wide, blacks have formed neighborhood watches, unarmed patrols, community fight back and "Take Back the Streets" groups. In the short term, they have been effective in reducing crime and driving dope peddlers from projects and apartment buildings, and in closing rock houses. But their efforts have been too diffused and unfocused. What is needed is a broad umbrella organization within African-American communities to coordinate anti-crime and community improvement actions—a Community Protection Council.

The Councils could educate and organize residents through on going door-to-door crime awareness drives and community forums. They could provide information and instruction to residents on methods and techniques to secure and protect their homes. They could also sponsor clean-up and anti-graffiti drives, plan sports and educational activities that provide youth with constructive outlets for their energies and talents, as well as foster pride in their neighborhoods.

They could conduct Positive Black Parenting Workshops that

teach and reinforce Afrocentric values of discipline, respect for elders, assistance to the infirm, family co-operation, work sharing and responsibility both in and outside the home, as well as African and African-American history and culture. The Councils would also demand that public school teachers and administrators support this approach to education and value training.

Outside the community, the Councils could be a powerful force to pressure local and public officials to reallocate private funds and tax monies for community events, social services, recreation, job development, skills training and career planning centers. The Councils should lobby for greater funding for financial compensation, counseling, medical and psychological treatment programs for the victims of both street and business crime.

With African-Americans soon comprising more than fifty percent of the American prison population, the black community has a tremendous stake in prison reform. The Councils could call for an end to the warehousing of prisoners, demanding instead that non-violent offenders be assigned to treatment and rehabilitation centers that provide job training, education, counseling programs and social services to prepare them for productive re-entrance into society.

There is also room for innovation. A Fine/Option Program could be imposed for minor property and drug abuse crimes. Offenders would pay a sum of money based on a sliding income scale. If unable to pay, they would be "sentenced" to non-residential detention to discharge their fine by working with a neighborhood organization. This program differs from the traditional penal community service work in three ways.

First, court supervised assignments are almost always "make work" jobs like cleaning the sides of freeways or painting grafitti. The aim is basically punitive, not community service and involvement. Second, the funds collected through the Fine/Option Program would be used to fund treatment, rehabilitation, community job and skill training programs, and not to bloat the budgets of police and courts. Most importantly, the program would not be the exclusive monopoly of wealthy white-collar criminals but open to all. This is why the program to be effective must be run jointly by the Council representatives and local court administrators. (3)

Since much of the violence among African-Americans stems from "petty" disputes, antagonism or insults, mediation and negotiation are tools that could be effective in saving lives. The Council could also establish Community Adult and Youth Panels with neutral hearing referees who would listen to complaints from the two (or more) disputants and seek a compromise. Mediation and negotiation could also be used to settle minor property crimes.

Community Protection Councils could be designed to ensure equal protection under the law. They could educate the public about how leniency toward corporate lawlessness directly breeds street lawlessness among young blacks. They would demand that the criminal justice system apply fair and equal standards to rich and poor alike.

Police-Community Partnerships

"I decided it was easier to educate the kids than incarcerate them," says Wayne Barton, a young black officer with the Boca Raton, Florida police department. He is a cop who not only cares about his community but also understands it. He knows that fighting crime does not only mean making arrests. Barton knows that for law enforcement to be truly effective the community must be on his side.

He will not get that support through harassment, abuse, victimization, deadly force, dragnets, street sweeps, roadblocks, or illegal arrests. He will only get the respect and cooperation of the community if he administers the law fairly and justly. Barton and the police officers who operate in the African-American community must be accountable to that community. A judge in Chicago indicated that 95 percent of the defendants in his court did not possess a high school diploma and had not attended church services or Sunday school.

Barton spends long hours working with the community out of uniform in after school tutoring, parenting, and drop-out programs. He is a founder of the community based "I Have a

)ream" Foundation that guarantees free college tuition to any 'outh from the Dixie Manor housing project who successfully ompletes high school. (4)

In African-American communities from Harlem to Compton, California, the police departments that have made a sincere attempt to work in partnership with the community have succeeded 1 reducing crime and the fears and tensions of the residents. The ·artnership can only work if police are willing to make the follow-1g changes:

—-Patrol officers and local police administrators ideally hould live in the community, and have strong personal and social les to the community. If not, they must be required to undergo 1tense, long term counseling, education and training on African-American lifestyles, history, culture, politics, community structure, nd social relations.

—Establish and enforce a firm policy against illegal arrests, .arassment and abuse. Any violation of the policy by an officer vould result in immediate discipline or firing.

—Demilitarize their ranks. This means no displays of heavy veapontry, air gunships, tanks and battering rams, or wearing of aramilitary uniforms and insignias. A total ban on the use of dead-y force unless an officer is in a genuine life threatening situation.

—A Police-Community Review Board, with full power to 1onitor and change police procedures and practices that violate 1dividual rights or are racially abusive in African-American com-1unities. It is crucially important to make the distinction here be-ween a fully independent Police-Community Review Board and 1e Police Commissions (or even Review Boards) that exist in many ities. Too often they merely serve as agencies that rubber stamp olice policies. Needless to say, a Police Review Board to be effec-ve must play a critical and impartial watchdog role in investigat-1g police misconduct.

Law enforcement cannot be effective until it shows a human-tic and not a punitive face in African-American communities. Of-cer Barton states, "You have to go way beyond traditional police work here."(5)

Education and Media Task Forces

In America, public education and the media have two problems in common. Both have failed to enlighten and inform their constituents about race and class oppression in America. And both have severely damaged the African-American image and self-image.

Black parents and organizations must continue to demand that the school systems educate or re-educate administrators and teachers in African-American history, culture, values, standards and family life. School districts must plan curriculum, make teacher assignments and choose texts and programs jointly with parent councils. The schools must be twenty-four hour resource centers for the community for meetings, events and community activities.

An education task force must focus especially on young black males. They are the prime victims of the repressive and neglectful social policies of the past decade. They must not be written off as the "lost generation." To instill pride, personal and social consciousness in young black men, black educators, Haki Madhubuti and Jawanza Kunjufu have suggested a rites of passage educational and developmental process. (6)

A Media Task Force has a similar job. It must demand that commercial broadcasters adopt a strong code of ethics. In the electronic media, the aim is to replace the carnage, mayhem and vice that currently pass for entertainment with more public affairs and educational programming. A strong push must be made for truth in advertising that promotes wholesome personal values and social concerns rather than greed, acquisition and cut-throat competition.

Finally, the Task Force must pressure the media to end the stereotyping of African-Americans. The Task Force must demand that TV, radio and newspapers present news, features and special reports on the positive accomplishments and activities of black professional and working people. With the young this is particular ly critical; if the media can show black kids spread-eagled on the ground, they can also show them going to school, planning careers, winning academic awards, and achieving as workers and in the professions.

When African-Americans forcefully demand media fairness and accuracy they can get results. In Miami, Summit 2000, a coalition of black community groups pressured the local ABC affiliate WSVN-TV to drop its highly rated Crime Check," a live nightly scene-of- the-crime feature. The group charged that nearly all the criminals shown were black.

"Too often reporters are insensitive or ill-informed about the black community," said Summit leader, Johnnie McMillan, "and consequently report inaccurate information." Small victories to be sure, but victories nonetheless that do serve as solid models for future action by a Media Task Force. (7)

Anti-Drug Networks

The drug plague is the single greatest cause of the escalation of crime and violence among African-Americans during the past decade. It will require the greatest attention of African-Americans. Drug abuse can only be combatted by recognizing that it is a social and health problem. Blacks, like white Americans, take drugs to escape personal pain, problems, and pressures of daily life. Unlike the white middle and upper-classes, they also take drugs to escape the special stress of racial and class oppression. They are victims and they can be helped by first looking at the past.

During the late 1950s and 1960s, the Nation of Islam proved that drug addiction and drug-related crime could be reduced among blacks. Malcolm X explained that there were no miracles or magic formulas in the Muslim rehabilitation program:

Our cure program's first major ingredient was the painfully patient work of Muslims who previously were junkies themselves. In the ghetto's dope jungle the Muslim ex-junkies would fish out addicts who knew them back in those days. Then with an agonizing patience that might span anywhere from a few months to a year, our ex-junky Muslims would conduct the addicts through the

Muslim six point therapeutic program.

The addict first was brought to admit to himself that he was an addict. Secondly, he was taught why he used narcotics. Third, he was shown that there was a way to stop addiction. Fourth, the addict's shattered self-image and ego were built up until the addict realized that he had, within, the self-power to end his addiction. Fifth, the addict voluntarily underwent a cold turkey break with drugs. Sixth, finally cured, now an ex-addict completes the cycle by 'fishing' up other addicts whom he knows, and supervising their salvaging."(8)

Several national black organizations borrowed from this model. The SCLC targeted six cities for its "Wings of Hope" program. It relied on church leaders to educate parishioners and their families about drug abuse, counseling and gang violence. The Muslim Dope Busters has rid housing projects in Washington, D.C. and New York of dope peddlers. They also try to politically educate addicts and ex-addicts to the damage their drug use does to themselves and the community.

A growing number of social support groups composed of recovering addicts and drug abuse professionals use the same approach as the Nation of Islam. These groups treat drug addiction as a disease and the individual as a victim of personal misfortune or social abuse. Wherever the education and treatment approach has been seriously tried, it has been successful.

The Muslim approach also makes good economic sense. The Treatment Outcome Prospective Study tracked more than 10,000 drug users in residential and outpatient treatment programs nationwide for five years. After one year, the former addicts had higher incomes, better skills and stable families.

Jailing addicts costs taxpayers ten times more than putting them in treatment programs. A three-month outpatient treatment program costs taxpayers about $600 per addict. The savings: $1,600 in reduced welfare and Medicaid costs and $1,300 in law enforcement expenditures. For a fraction of the $100 billion that the state and federal government will be required to spend to build more prisons, they could treat every hard core addict that wants help.

And many do want help. U.S. Senate Judiciary Committee chairman Joseph Biden, estimates that each day 56,000 addicts seek treatment. They will be turned away from the few treatment centers open for lack of staff or space. It takes little imagination to figure out that they will continue to roam the streets engaging in illegal activities to support their habits.

The 56,000 addicts who want help cannot look to the Bush anti-drug strategists. The $7.8 billion Bush allocated in the 1990-1991 budget to fight the "war on drugs" will go for more judges, law enforcement personnel and prisons, not treatment. The war will be lost before the first shot is fired.(9)

Finally, Anti-Drug Networks must confront a troubling question. With drug sales a multi-billion dollar business, no anti-drug campaign or program can fully succeed until the profit is taken out of the trade. One way is decriminalization. There are certainly compelling arguments for changing the laws. This might reduce the death toll from drug violence, identify and assist drug abusers, and rechannel millions now spent on police and prisons into drug research, education and treatment.

But there are compelling arguments against decriminalization. Is it in the best interest of African-Americans to legalize a substance that disorientates an individual's consciousness, impairs health and could result in death? Critics of decriminalization say that it makes no difference whether addicts get their fixes from the government or the street corner pusher. They will still rob, cheat or prostitute themselves to get money to buy drugs.

The cost to the community would be the possibility of further pain and suffering within families, more crime, and less political and economic independence and self-reliance. The high disease and death rates among African-Americans, much of it caused by drugs, could soar higher if drugs were legally sold.(10)

The jury is still out on decriminalization of hard drugs. Yet it is an issue that must be faced. For now Anti-Drug Networks must continue to insist that the drug users be decriminalized. And that means treating them as victims not criminals.

Jobs And Income Not Jails

During a citizen's forum the author once attended, the mayor of the local city spoke in glowing terms about the great things his administration had done to reduce crime. The mayor, who happens to be black, told the audience that the city had hired more police, increased funding, added more patrols, and beefed up its arsenal of weapons. The audience, nearly all-black, politely applauded.

Afterwards, the mayor was asked if he really believed that this had put a stop to crime. He thought for a moment and then said: "You know when crime actually dropped is when they put in the discount department store." The department store provided jobs for dozens of neighborhood youth.

It is no coincidence that crime is at its lowest when the government or major industry puts the masses to work. The Depression-Era New Deal programs such as the Civilian Conservation Corps (CCC), Works Progress Administration and the National Recovery Administration provided jobs and income to millions of destitute Americans. During the World War II military build-up, the industrialists received massive government contracts to keep factories running at full tilt.

Lyndon Johnson's Great Society programs and the CETA programs of the Jimmy Carter years gave the poor employment, welfare and educational opportunities. Nearly every Democratic President from Roosevelt to Carter claimed to support full employment as a means of bringing the poor into the economic mainstream. But no Democratic administration has followed through and implemented permanent, full employment programs.(11)

In the Reagan-Bush era of supply-side economics the chances of full employment are non-existent. This does not mean that community groups and political organizations should not continue to press for a national full employment policy. Crime reduction among African-Americans and the poor directly hinges on jobs and income for all.

Even inadequate and poorly designed welfare programs that boost income and lessen the poverty burden have marginally reduced certain types of crime among the poor. One study has shown that an increase of only $10 in Aid to Families with Dependent Children decreased the homicide rate by 1.38%, the rape rate 5.50%, and burglary rate by 10.5%. (12)

Despite the wastefulness and mismanagement of some CETA programs during the Carter years, many ex-prisoners were helped by CETA. In St. Louis, the CETA Prime Sponsor Program established 13 Criminal Justice Agencies. More than 750 felony offenders were given job and skill training through these agencies, as well as counseling and other support services. Forty percent of the trainees eventually were placed in public and private sector jobs. All for a total cost of only $100,000.

The reality is that only government can provide adequate jobs and income in African-American communities. Since world War II, government, not private industry, has been responsible for most of the job growth. The only exception was the period from 1947 to 1957 when corporate job growth (53 percent) slightly exceeded government growth . Operating in today's era of scarcity, mergers and technical specialization, big business is simply incapable of providing jobs to any but the most skilled, technically trained workers. (13)

Government created jobs are not charity, nor will they encourage more dependence. African-Americans pay billions in taxes and fees. If the government can bail out Chrylser, Lockheed, failed Saving & Loans, the Russian and Polish economy, and squander billions on obsolete weapons, it can provide jobs, income and services to African-Americans.

A first step then is a government-sponsored national youth service similar to the CCC programs of the 1930s. Such a service should not be "make work" programs but would be designed to train the young in literacy, mechanical and technical skills to meet the competitive standards of industry.

The government, in partnership with community organiza-

103

tions, could also establish publicly-run nonprofit corporations. They could be funded by a combination of tax subsidies, credits, direct payments, and through a corporate unemployment tax specifically to hire the unemployed for social, public and cultural works projects.

Income maintenance is also vital for the stabilization of black females on welfare. The current jumble of rules and regulations each state uses to determine family assistance must be scrapped. It does nothing but encourage black dependence, split families, force males out of the home and provide only subsistence income.

The better model for the nation is the Massachusetts program, "Education and Training Choices." The program does not coerce welfare mothers to take sweatshop jobs at minimum wages, with no child care. Rather it provides education, counseling, job training and work experience for the modern job market. The progress of the participants is professionally supervised and monitored during training.(13)

In addition to full employment, welfare and educational reform, national health insurance, affordable moderate and low income housing, and a national child care system will enable millions of African-Americans to feel more secure in their person and property.

Finally, African-Americans must play a major role in their own social and economic uplift. The estimated $150 billion blacks annually spend on goods and services can serve as a foundation for viable business and community self-help programs. The NAACP, SCLC, PUSH, black fraternities, sororities, professional and business organizations have already recognized the potential. They have launched innovative programs to provide jobs, training, recreation, scholarships, male role modeling and support services for young blacks.

A cautionary note must be inserted here. Neither self-help programs nor black businesses alone can nor should be expected to provide mass employment, and cure the chronic, deep-seated social and educational needs, of African-Americans. Still, self-help is vital because it serves as a transitional program to counter government inaction, and encourages black initiative, independence and empowerment.

These solutions are not meant to be the last word. They are only steps along the way, but they are crucial steps. Safe streets in African-American communities can never be completely attained until African-Americans confront their oppressors and not each other.

Conclusion

By the end of the day on July 17, 1988, Jeffrey Ellerbe had robbed two restaurants and a suburban motorist in the Washington, D.C. area. Ellerbe fit the image many Americans have of a criminal. He was young, unemployed, a cocaine addict, and most importantly, he was black. Worse, Ellerbe committed his robberies in a city that has become synonymous with black crime in America.

But there was a twist. Ellerbe did not rob because he was needy, or because he was a malicious person. Nor did he commit his crimes to feed his drug habit. He robbed because he wanted to get help for his addiction. Before he began his crime spree, Ellerbe had called fifteen different drug treatment centers in the city seeking admittance. Each one told him they were filled and could not accept him. Desperate for help, Ellerbe pulled the robberies to get arrested. He figured this was the only way he would get any treatment.(1)

He was not a criminal, but the desperate circumstances of his life had made him one. Ellerbe will have a police record. He is another of the one out of four young black males either in jail, on probation or parole. In the coming years, the ranks of America's prisons will swell with thousands more young men like Ellerbe. They will deal drugs, join gangs and kill each other and innocent bystanders with seeming impunity.

They will continue to be the subject of sensationalist and racist-tinged crime exposés by the press. They will continue to be convenient foils used by many public officials to browbeat an anxious public into approving bigger and bigger police and prisons budgets. Many Americans will continue to be willing to discard constitutional liberties in the belief that they are to blame for the nation's crime, drugs and violence.

Americans can never understand the Ellerbes' that walk their streets until they first shed some myths. The crimes they commit cannot be separated from American society. Blacks do not kill because they enjoy violence. They do not steal because they are part of a subculture of poverty. They do not deal drugs because they have low self-esteem and aspirations.

But they do see the justice system prescribe one standard of punishment for the rich and another for the poor. They do learn values and violence from TV. They do mirror the corrupt ethics of many businessmen and politicians who place a high premium on cut throat competition and materialism.

The Ellerbes' of America are the victims of the nation's shameful and continuing legacy of slavery, segregation, institutional racism, exploitation, violence and greed. They are the victims of the failed economic and social policies of the Reagan-Bush era that gutted job, education and social programs for the working class and the poor.

I have attempted to explain some of the causes of crime by challenging many of the stereotypes about African-Americans. I have also tried to present some immediate solutions that might lessen the fears of many Americans of black crime. But as Kenneth Clarke warns, Americans must realize that: "Mugged communities, mugged neighborhoods, and mugged schools spawn urban muggers."

Crime, no matter whether committed with a pen or gun, in the streets or the suites, will continue to be America's scourge until the battle against racism, economic inequality, and social injustice is won. African-Americans have a huge stake in that struggle. For victory in this fight will end the mugging of black America.

Notes

INTRODUCTION

Abbreviations: Los Angeles Times (LAT)
                   New York Times (NYT)
                   Wall Street Journal (WSJ)

1. *The Miami Herald*, September 14, 1990.

2. "Statistical Abstract of the United States" (Washington, D.C., 1989) 160; *LAT*, February 27, 1990, April 23, 1990.

3. *Law Enforcement Assistance Administration*, "Black Crime: A Police View" (October, 1977) 25-26; *Atlanta Constitution*, August 17, 1990 (advertisement); John E. Conklin, *Criminology* (New York: Macmillian, 1981) 16; Wade W. Nobles and Lawford L. Goddard, "Drugs in the African-American Community: A Clear and Present Danger in National Urban League," *The State of Black America 1989* (New York: National Urban League, 1989) 174.

4. Douglas G. Glasgow, *The Black Underclass* (New York: Vintage Press, 1981) 104.

5. Darnell F. Hawkins, "Black and White Imprisonment," *Crime and Social Justice*, 24 (Summer, 1985) 205; Bernard D. Headley, "'Black on Black' Crime: The Myth and the Reality," *Crime and Social Justice*, 20 (Fall 1984) 57-59; Robert M. O'Brien, "The Interracial Nature of Violent Crimes," *American Journal of Sociology*, Vol. 92, No. 4 (January, 1987) 817-835.

6. U.S. Department of Justice, Report to the Nation on Crime and

Justice, (Washington, D.C.: Government Printing Office, 1988) 121; *LAT*, May 24, 1990.

7. *LAT*, May 6, 1990; *Time Magazine*, March 13, 1989; Andrew Hacker, "Getting Used To Mugging," *New York Review of Books*, April 19, 1973, 24.

8. Leon Kamin, "Are There Genes For Crime?" *Science for the People*, (July/August, 1986) 8-10; David Stratman, "Thinking About Crime," (review), *Crime and Social Justice*, 4 (Fall-Winter, 1975) 60.

9. *LAT*, March 15, 1990.

10. Ramsey Clark, *Crime in America* (New York: Simon and Schuster, 1970) 57.

1. LEGACY OF SLAVERY

1. *LAT*, July 18, 1990.

2. John Hope Franklin, *From Slavery to Freedom* (New York: Vintage Press, 1969) 11-22; Melville J. Herskovits, *The Myth of the Negro Past* (Boston: Beacon Press, 1967) 158-167; Andrew Billingsley, *Black Families in White America* (Englewood Cliifs, N.J.: Prentice-Hall, 1968) 40-48. Also see, Chancellor Williams, *The Destruction of Black Civilization* (Chicago: Third World Press, 1974).

3. Paul Bohannan, *African Homicide and Suicide* (Princeton: Princeton University Press, 1960) 236-251.

4. Andrew Billingsley, *Black Families in White America*, 51.

5. August Meier and Elliot Rudwick, *From Plantation to Ghetto* (New York: Hill & Wang, 1966) 57-60; Herbert Aptheker, *American Negro Slave Revolts* (New York: International Publishers, 1970) 66.

6. *The Constitution of the United States* (New York: Doubleday, 1960) 41, 51; Leon Litwak, *North of Slavery* (Chicago: University of Chicago Press, 1970) 3-63, 95.

7. Andrew Billingsley, 56; Herbert G. Gutman, *The Black Family* in *Slavery and Freedom 1750-1925* (New York: Random House, 1976)

158; Frederick Douglass, *The Life and Times of Frederick Douglass* (New York: Collier Books, 1962) 148

8. Herbert G. Gutman, Ibid., 339; Thomas F. Pettigrew, *A Profile of Negro Americans* (Princeton: D. Van Nostrand Co., 1964)147-148, 293.

9. Robert Lefcourt (ed.) *Law Against the People* (New York: Vintage Books, 1971) 192-194; Mary Frances Berry, *Black Resistance/White Law* (New York: Meredith Corporation, 1971) 103-135.

10. Darnell F. Hawkins, "Black-White Imprisonment," 206; John Dittmer, *Black Georgia in the Progressive Era*, 1900-1920 (Urbana: University of Illinois Press, 1977) 81-87.

11. John Dittmer, *Black Georgia*, 50-71; E. Franklin Frazier, *The Negro In The United States* (New York: The Macmillan Co., 1957) 213-228.

12. Bernard Peyton Chamberlain, "The Negro and Crime in Virginia" (Richmond: Phelps-Stokes Fellowship Papers, 1936) 100-101; Thomas F. Pettigrew, *A Profile of Negro Americans*, 143.

13. Lawrence E. Gary and Lee P. Brown, *Crime and It's Impact on the Black Community* (Washington, D.C.: Howard University Press, 1975) 42-44.

14. James Baldwin, *Nobody Knows My Name* excerpted in Eric and Mary Josephson (eds.) *Man Alone* (New York: Dell Publishing Co., 1962) 353-354.

15. Richard Wright, *Native Son* (New York: The New American Library, 1964) 320.

16. E. Franklin Frazier, The Negro Family in the United States (Chicago: University of Chicago Press, 1966) 228-229.

17. Thurgood Marshall "The Gestapo in Detroit," *The Crisis* (August, 1943) 232-233; John Hope Franklin, *From Slavery to Freedom* (New York: Vintage Books, 1969) 597-598.

18. Jose Torres, *Fear and Fire* (New York: New American Library, 1989) 32; Frantz Fanon, *Black Skin, White Masks* (New York: Grove

Press, 1967) 139.

19. Frantz Fanon, *The Wretched of the Earth* (New York: Grove Press, 1966) 248-249.

20. Leonard Berkowitz, "The Study of Urban Violence," *The American Behavioral Scientist*, Vol. 11, No. 4 (March-April, 1968) 14-17; Thomas F. Pettigrew, *A Profile of Negro Americans*, 151-152.

21. Claude Brown, *Manchild in the Promised Land* (New York: The Macmillan Co., 1965) 312.

22. Carl Ginsberg details how the media and government policy makers used the Moynihan Report to savage African-Americans see, "Race and Media: The Enduring Life of the Moynihan Report" (New York: Institute for Media Analysis, Inc., 1989).

23. John Allen, Phillip Heymann and Diane Hall, *Assault with a Deadly Weapon: The Autobiography of a Street Criminal* (New York: Pantheon, 1977) 8; Robert J. Sampson, "Urban Black Violence," *American Journal of Sociology*, Vol. 93, No. 2 (September, 1987) 370-373.

24. Ralph Ellison, *Invisible Man* (New York: New American Library, 1952) 7-8; Quoted in Charles E. Silberman, *Criminal Violence, Criminal Justice* (New York: Random House, 1978) 200.

25. Douglas G. Glasgow exposes the many flaws in the "Subculture of Poverty" theory in "The Black Underclass in Perspective," *State of Black America, 1987* (New York: The National Urban League, 1988) 129-135 ; E. Franklin Frazier, *Black Bourgeoisie* (New York: Collier Books, 1962) 25.

26. Bebe Moore Campbell, "Success Beyond the Open Door," *Black Enterprise*, August, 1990, 113; Douglas Glasgow, "The Black Underclass in Perspective," 133-134.

27. Russell Middleton, "Alienation, Race, and Education," *American Sociological Review*, Vol. 28 (December, 1963) 973-977; Claude McKay, *Harlem: Negro Metropolis* (New York: Harcourt Brace Jovanovich, 1968) 112.

28. Richard M. McGaney, "Economic Conditions, Organization, and Urban Crime," in Albert J. Reiss and Michael Tanny, *Communities and Crime* (Chicago: University of Chicago Press, 1986) 253; Ulf Hannerz, "What Ghetto Males are Like: Another Look," in *Afro-American Anthropology* (New York: Free Press, 1970) 160-161.

2. QUEST FOR POWER

1. *WSJ*, March 1, 1990; *LAT*, June 12, 1990; Time, May 25, 1987, 15-20.

2. *LAT*, May 9, 1990, July 21, 1990; March 9, 1990. Robert Lekachman details how Reagan's economic policies encouraged the rich and powerful to pillage the national treasury, see *Greed Is Not Enough: Reaganomics* (New York: Pantheon, 1982).

3. John Hagan and Alberto Polloni, "Sentencing White Collar Offenders," *Criminology*, Vol. 24, No.4 (November, 1986) 618-620; Michael L. Benson, et.al., District Attorney's and Corporate Crime: Suveying the Prosecutorial Gatekeepers," *Criminology*, Vol. 26, No. 3 (1988) 505-515.

4. *LAT*, August 12, 1990; Stuart L. Hills (ed.) *Corporate Violence* (Totowa, N.J.: Rowman & Littlefield, 1987) 1-8.

5. The Federalist No. 10 in Clinton Rossiter (ed.) *The Federalist Papers* (New York: New American Library, 1961) 79; Christopher Collier and James Lincoln Collier discuss at length the Founding Fathers preoccupation with class and race politics at the Constitutional Convention of 1787, see *Decision In Philadelphia* (New York: Ballantine Books, 1987). 183-205.

6. Kenneth Cloke, "The Economic Basis of Law and State," in Robert Lefcourt, *Law Against the People* (New York: Vintage Books, 1971) 72-74; Matthew Josephson, The Robber Barons.

7. Richard F. Sullivan, "The Economics of Crime," *Crime and Delinquency*, 19 (April 1973) 139-144; James Comer, *Beyond Black and White* (New York: Quadrangle Books, 1972) 54.

8. Ramsey Clark, *Crime in America* , 37-38.

9. Quoted in Garth L. Mangum and Stephen F. Seninger, *Coming of Age in the Ghetto* (Baltimore: Johns Hopkins University Press, 1978), 78-81; *LAT*, July 18, 1990.

10. Douglas G. Glasgow, *The Black Underclass*, 90-91; Michael Hughes and David H. Demo, "Self-Perceptions of Black Americans: Self-Esteem and Personal Efficacy," *American Journal of Sociology*, Vol. 91, No. 1 (July 1989) 132157; Benjamin E. Mays and Joseph Nicholson, "The Genius of the Negro Church," in Hart M. Nelson (ed.), *The Black Church in America* (New York: Basic Books, 1971) 28.

11. Kenneth B. Clark & Mamie P. Clark, *Racial Identification and Preferences in Negro Children*. Readings in Social Psychology (New York: Holt Inc., 1947); Richard Kluger, *Simple Justice* (New York: Alfred A. Knopf, Co., 1973); Adelbert H. Jenkins, *The Psychology of the Afro-American* (New York: Pergamon Press, 1982) 24-25.

12. Adelbert H. Jenkins, Ibid. 25-31; Michael McMillan, "The Doll Test Studies—From Cabbage Patch to Self-Concept," *The Journal of Black Psychology*, February 1988, Vol. 14, No. 2, 69-72; Edward J. Barn, "The Black Community as the Source of Positive Self-Concept for Black Children" in Reginald Jones (ed.), *Black Psychology* (New York: Harper & Row, 1980) 110-111.

13. James Banks, "Racial Prejudice and the Black Self-Concept," in James A. Banks and Jean D. Grambs, *Black Self-Concept* (New York: McGraw-Hill, 1972) 14-18; Dante P. Ciochetti, "CBE Interviews: Kenneth B. Clark," *Bulletin of the Council for Basic Education*, 14 (November 1969) 15-16; The Rand Report is entitled "Multiplying Inequalities: The Effects of Race, Social Class and Tracking Opportunities to Learn Mathematics and Science," excerpts in *Los Angeles Sentinel*, September 27, 1990.

14. Adelbert H. Jenkins, *The Psychology of the Afro-American*, 27; Roy Lotz, *Juvenile Delinquency and Juvenile Justice* (New York: Random House, 1985) 101; Richard M. McGahey, "Economic Conditions, Organization, and Urban Crime" in Albert J. Reiss and Albert Tanny, *Communities and Crime* (Chicago: University of Chicago

Press, 1986) 251.

15. Richard Wright, *Native Son*, 327; Quoted in Rick Telander "Senseless," *Sports Illustrated*, May 14, 1990 Reprint NPN.

16. Quoted in Eric and Mary Josephson, *Man Alone* (New York: Dell, 1962) 344.

17. Lawrence E. Gary and Lee P. Brown, "Crime and Its Impact on the Black Community," 6-7.

18. *U.S. News & World Report*, March 12, 1990; "U.S. Department of Commerce, Statistical Abstract of the United States" (Washington, D.C., GPO. 1989) 138-139, 381;U. S. Bureau of the Census, "Current Population Reports," series P-60, No. 157; *LAT*, July 29, 1990; David H. Swinton, "Summary of the Economic Status of Black Americans During the 1980's," *Black Excellence*, Vol.2, No. 4, 47-50; *LAT*, March 21, 1990, July 18, 1990.

19. Two useful books for understanding the current crisis of American capitalism are, Michael Barone, *Our Country: The Shaping of America From Roosevelt to Reagan* (New York: The Free Press, 1990) and Robert Heilbroner, *The Limits of American Capitalism* (New York: Harper Torchbooks, 1965); *LAT*, July 15, 1990.

20. The Crime trends in the 1970s as reflected in the FBI's UCR's are summarized in U.S. Department of Justice, "Report to the Nation on Crime and Justice" (Washington, D.C.: GPO, 1988) 13-15; also Louis Lieberman and Alexander B. Smith assess poverty and crime trends during the same period, see "Crime Rates and Poverty—A Reexamination," *Crime and Social Justice* , No. 25 (Summer 1987) 169-171; "Unemployment and Crime," House Judiciary Committee Hearings, September 27, 1978 (Washington, D.C.: GPO, 1978) 30-35; U.S. Bureau of Justice Statistics, "Prisoners in State and Federal Institutions on December 31," Annual; 1985 (Washington, D.C.: GPO, 1986); Statistical Abstract of the United States, 165.

21. Charles Silberman, "Criminal Violence, Criminal Justice," 161; Manning Marable, "Toward Black Empowerment," *African Com-*

mentary, May 1990, 17-18; Darnell F. Hawkins, "Black and White Homicide Differentials," *Criminal Justice and Behavior*, Vol 10, No. 4 (December 1983) 429-430.

22. Robert Lefcourt, "Law Against the People," 28; Richard M. Mc-Gahey, "Economic Conditions, Organization, and Urban Crime," 250.

3. THE MUGGING OF THE BLACK IMAGE

1. *Newsweek*, July 23, 1990; *NYT*, August 15, 1990.

2. Southern racists were not the ones who engaged in vicious anti-black press and literary caricaturing during the late 19th Century. Some of the most respected and scholarly academics and professionals commonly engaged in racist stereotyping in books, magazines and newspapers. For example, Walter Wilcox in the keynote address to the American Association of Social Sciences blamed black crime on defective family life and training. Among the family "defects" he listed were laziness, drunkeness and sexual promiscuity, see George M. Frederickson, *The Black Image in the White Mind* (New York: Harper & Row, 1971)198-319; Herbert G. Gutman, *The Black Family in Slavery and Freedom, 1750-1925*, 538.

3. Rayford Logan, "The Negro as Portrayed in Representative Northern Magazines and Newspapers," in Barry N. Schwartz and Robert Disch, *White Racism* (New York: Dell Publishing Co., 1970) 392-398; Quoted in Louis R. Harlan, *Booker T. Washington* (New York: Oxford University Press, 1983) 319.

4. Kelly Miller, Radicals & Conservatives (Reprint 1908, New York: Schocken Books, 1968) 85, 86. Thomas Dixon's racist novels remained a smashing commercial success with the general public well into the 1920s, see Dixon's "The Leopard's Spots: A Study in Popular Racism" in Barry N, Schwartz and Robert Disch, *White Racism*, 111-120.

5. Various editions of the *NYT, LAT, NY Post*, and *Washington Post*; *Newsweek*, July 23, 1990; *Amsterdam News*, July 21, 1990; *WSJ*,

August 21, 1990.

6. *LAT*, March 23, 1990, July 18,1990.

7. Ben Bagdikian, *The Media Monopoly* (Boston: Beacon Press, 1987) 4, 21; "Statistical Abstract of the United States," 566-568; *Lies Of Our Times*, May 1990, 6.

8. Ronald Barri Flowers, *Minorities and Criminality* (Westport, Ct.: Greenwood Press, 1988) 30-31. Aware of the glaring omissions in the FBI's Uniform Crime Reports, many criminologists rely on the Bureau of Justice Statistic's National Crime Survey for a more accurate picture of street crime. For a comparison of the UCR and the National Crime Survey see Department of Justice, "Report to the Nation on Crime and Justice," 1988, 11.

9. Kevin N. Wright, *The Great American Crime Myth* (New York: Praeger, 1985); Roy Lotz (et.al), *Juvenile Delinquency and Juvenile Justice* (New York: Random House, 1985) 48.

10. James Aronson shows how TV managers and newspaper editors continually inject their pro-business bias into the news, see Packaging the News (New York: International Publishers, 1971). Michael Parenti warns that with the move toward privatization of the media in Eastern European new reports there will soon reflect the same pro-capitalist, anti-poor and working class slant, see "Free Market Media In Eastern Europe," *Lies Of Our Times*, September 1990. 11-12; *LAT*, September 22, 1990.

11. *LAT*, July 8, 1990.

12. *Newsweek*, January 29, 1990; *The New Republic*, February 12, 1990, 9; *The Nation*, "Crack in the Washington Culture," February 19, 1990, 238-240; *Amsterdam News*, July 21, 1990; *LAT*, August 20, 1990.

13. Charles E. Silberman, *Criminal Violence, Criminal Justice*, 212; Gordon L. Berry, "Television and the Black Child: Some Psychological Imperatives," *Reflections on Black Psychology* (Washington, D.C.: University Press of America, 1979) 109-110; Gregg Barak, "Behind Black Crime," *Southern Changes* (December 1986) 8.

14. Gordon L. Berry, Ibid., 111-112; "Violence and the Media," in the report issued by the National Commission on the Causes and Prevention of Violence (Washington, D.C., GPO, 1969) 251-252; *L.A. Sentinel*, July 19, 1990.

15. John Langone, *The Causes of Violence* (New York: Little, Brown and Co., 1984) 49-51; *U.S. News & World Report* ; A Nigerian visitor watching a TV western for the first time purportedly exclaimed, "I did not realize that you valued life so little in the West." Marshall McLuhan, *Understanding the Media* (New York: New American Library, 1964) 278.

4. THE DOPING OF THE GHETTO

1. LAT, April 22, 1990.

2. Marsha Rosenbaum, *Just Say What?* (San Francisco: National Council on Crime and Delinquency, 1990) 5-7; LAT, April 20, 1990; Jeanette Covington, "Self-Esteem and Deviance: The Effects of Race and Gender," Criminology, Vol. 24, No. 1 (January 1986) 105-138.

3. Dennis Desmond and Clarence Lusane, *Stopping Bush's Drug War* (Washington, D.C.: Fighting Word's Publications, 1990) 5, 7-8; LAT, May 21, 1990.

4. LAT, July 15, 1990; Desmond and Lusane, Ibid, 17, 18: LAT, August 24, 1990.

5. LAT, March 20, 1990.

6. Benjamin P. Bowser, "Crack and Aids: An Ethnographic Impression," Journal of the National Medical Association, Vol. 81, No. 5. The only evidence to support the notion of criminal empires in black neighborhoods is the word of a few federal prosecutors, see Stephen J. Brodt, "Controlling Organized Crime," Criminal Justice Abstracts, Vol. 2, No. 3 (1987) 269-300; NYT, August 11, 1990; Ebony, August 1989, 108.

7. LAT , March 20, 1990, March 22, 1990.

8. LAT, April 22, 1990; Douglas G. Glasgow, *The Black Underclass*, 96.

9. Beny J. Primm, "Drug Use: Special Implications for Black America," in State of Black America, 1988, 146-148.

10. Claude Brown, *Manchild in the Promised Land*, 263, 170.

11. Arnold Rampersad, *The Life of Langston Hughes*, Vol II, (New York: Oxford University Press, 1988) 362; Malcolm X, *The Autobiography of Malcolm X* (New York: Grove Press, 1965) 263.

12. U.S. News & World Report, March 12, 1990, 30-31; LAT, July 8, 1990.

13. LAT, March 22, 1990, April 22, 1990.

14. LAT, April 22, 1990.

15. Randolph N. Stone, "The War on Drugs," NBA Magazine, December 1989, 21; Ebony, "High Noon at the Housing Project," August, 1989, 130-132.

16. Washington Post, Sept 9, 1989.

17. Randolph N. Stone, Ibid. 34; LAT, August 7, 1990.

18. LAT, April 22, 1990, July 18, 1990.

5. THE COLLAPSE OF THE MOVEMENT

1. Washington Evening Star, August 29, 1963; New York Times, August 29, 1963.

2. Andrew Billingsley, "Black Families in a Changing Society," 97 in *The State of Black America 1988* (New York: National Urban League, 1989); Author interview with LAPD Sargeant, July 6, 1990.

3. Karl Marx labeled the marginalized underclass as the "lumpenproletariat." They often make their living off of street hustles and crime, and in revolutionary times can become either dedicated revolutionists or treacherous counter-revolutionaries. During the Paris Commune uprising they played both roles, see Alistair Horne, *The Fall of Paris* (New York: Penguin Books, 1981); Frantz Fanon, *The Wretched of the Earth*, (New York: Grove Press, 1966) 247, 250.

4. Malcolm X with Alex Haley, *The Autobiography of Malcolm X*, (New York: Grove Press, 1965) 265.

5. Malcolm X, *The Autobiography of Malcolm X*, 185.

6. George Jackson, *Soledad Brother* (New York: Bantom, 1970) 185.

7. Thomas Pettigrew, *Negro American Protest* , 166.

8. Martin Luther King, Jr., *Where Do We Go From Here: Chaos or Community?* (Boston: Beacon Press, 1968) 17.

9. Frederick Solomon, et al., "Civil Rights Activity and Reduction in Crime among Negroes," Archives of General Psychiatry, Vol. 12 (1965) 227-236.

10. Tom Hayden, *Rebellion in Newark* (New York: Vintage, 1967) 29-30.

11. Douglas G. Glasgow, *The Black Underclass*, 147, 151.

12. David Garrow, *The FBI and Martin Luther King Jr.*, (New York: Penguin Books, 1983); Baxter Smith, *The FBI Plot Against The Black Movement* (New York: Pathfinder Press, 1974) 14, 18. Also see, Kenneth O'Reilly, "Racial Matters," *The FBI's Secret File on Black America*, 1960-1972 (New York: Free Press, 1989).

13. William Junius Wilson, *The Declining Significance of Race* (Chicago: The University of Chicago Press, 1978) 113; James Ellis, "The Growing Gap Between the Haves and the Have-Nots," Business Week, March 14, 1988, 69.

14. Robert L. Allen details how the government and corporations succeeded in derailing black militancy after the urban rebellions, see *Black Awakening in Capitalist America* (New York: Doubleday, 1969). 108-206.

15. William Junius Wilson, Ibid. 91.

6. MYTHS AND LIES

1. Newsweek, January 22, 1990; LAT, May 11, 1990.

2. Statistical Abstract of the United States, 109th ed. (GPO. Washington, D.C.: GPO, 1989), 1179; U.S. Bureau of Justice Statistics, Capital Punishment, annual; Ronald Barri Flowers, *Minorities and Crime* (Westport, Ct.: Greenwood, 1988) 169-171; Alfred B. Heilbrun, Jr., et.al. "The Death Sentence in Georgia, 1974-1987," Criminal Justice and Behavior, Vol. 16, No.2 (June 1989) 139-154; NAACP Legal Defense Fund Bulletin..........: LAT, August 25, 1985.

3. LAT, June 4, 1990.

4. Tom Wicker, "Defending the Indigent in Capital Cases," Criminal Justice Ethics (Winter/Spring, 1983) 2.

5. LAT, March 23, 1990; May 11, 1990.

6. Nixon quote cited in Ofari's Bi-Monthly, Vol 1, No.6 (Summer, 1987) 12; Richard Lacayo, "Our Bulging Prisons," Time, May 29, 1989, 28-30; U. S. News & World Report., March 12, 1990; LAT, May 6, 1990; Steven Whitman, "The Crime of Black Imprisonment," Chicago Tribune, May 28, 1987; Statistical Abstract of the United States, 109th ed. .

7. Steven Whitman, Ibid.

8. Atlanta Journal and Constitution, August 16, 1990; LAT, May 10, 1990, April 22, 1990.

9. Charles Silberman, Criminal Violence, Criminal Justice (New York: Random House, 1978) 505; Claude Brown, *Manchild in the Promised Land*, 249.

10. LAT, May 6, 1990.

11. Richard D. Schwartz and Jerome H. Skolnick, "Two Studies of Legal Stigma," Social Problems, Vol. 10 (Fall, 1962) 133-138

12. Charles Silberman, Criminal Violence, Criminal Justice, 348-353.

13. Charles R. Key, "The Preventive Patrol Experiment," Crime Prevention Review , Vol 3, No.1 (October, 1975) 25-29.

14. Ed Cray, *The Enemy in the Streets*, (New York: Anchor Books,

43) 42; Ofari's Bi-Monthly, "The Mugging of America," Vol. 1, No. 6 (Summer, 1987) 13; LAT, April 22, 1990.

15. Ed Cray, *The Enemy in the Streets*, 188-207; *Report of the National Advisory Commission on Civil Disorders* (New York: Bantom Books, 1968) 368-373; Alexander Pisciatta argues that urban police departments in America historically have acted in the interests of the industrialists and the wealthy to repress minorities and labor, see "Police, Society, and Social Control," Criminal Justice Abstracts, Vol.14, No.4 (December 1982) 524-531; Arnold Binder and Laurie Fridell, "Lethal Force As a Police Response," Criminal Justice Abstracts, Vol. 16, No. 2 (June 1984) 260-264.

16. LAT, May 4, 1990.

17. Greg Barak, "The Myth and Reality of Black on Black Crime," Dialogue (Summer-Fall, 1988) 2-3; Newsweek, July 23, 1990.

18. Darnell F. Hawkins, "Devalued Lives and Racial Stereotypes," in Robert L. Hampton (ed.) *Violence in the Black Family* (Lexington, Ma.: D.C. Heath and Co., 1987) 194, 198-199;

19. Caramae Richey Mann, "Black Women Who Kill," in Robert L. Hampton (ed.) *Violence in the Black Family*, 180; Dallas Times Herald, August 19, 1990; LAT, August 25, 1990; Darnell F. Hawkins, "Black and White Homicide Differentials," Criminal Justice and Behavior, Vol. 10, No. 4 (December 1983) 420-421.

20. Harold E. Pepinsky and Paul Jesilow, *Myths That Cause Crime* (Washington, D.C.; Seven Locks Press, 1984) 88-89.

21. Candace Krulschnutt, et.al., "Causes of Violent Behavior," Criminology, Vol. 24, No.2, 1986 235-268; Andrew Hacker, "Getting Used To Mugging," New York Review of Books, April 19,1973.

22. Newsweek, April 16, 1984; Time, April 8, 1985.

7. SOLUTIONS

1. Lawrence E. Gary and Lee P. Brown, *Crime and Its Impact on the Black Community* (Washington, D.C., Howard University Press,

1975) 46-47. August Meier documents the strong influence the temperance and self-improvement movement had on African-Americans during the early years of the 20th Century in Negro Thought In America, 1880-1915 (Ann Arbor: University of Michigan Press, 1968) 135-136.

2. In These Times, February 6-12, 1985; Interview with Maulana Karenga, December 12, 1989.

3. Anne Newton details the progressive alternatives to incarceration in West Europe, Australia, and Japan that could easily be used in America, see "Alternatives To Imprisonment: An International Perspective," Criminal Justice Abstracts, Vol.13, No.1 (March, 1981) 134-145. Phillip Hager surveys the penal innovations some states have come up with to break the "crime-prison-more crime" cycle, "Upholding the Law in New Ways," LAT, May 15, 1990.

4. Parade Magazine, August 5, 1990 12-13

5. Compton, California and Harlem provide excellent examples of how black residents will co-operate with the police and the respect police receive from black residents when they enforce the law with fairness and sensitivity, see Gene Kaplan, "The Compton Police Department and Law Enforcement," Crime Prevention Review , Vol. 5, No.3 (April, 1978) 18-23; Stephen Lerner, The Police and the Black Community (New York: NYU Press, 1984) 210-223; Parade Magazine, August 5, 1990, 13.

6. Haki R. Madhubuti, The Black Male: Obsolete, Single, or Endangered? (Chicago: Third World Press, 1990); Jawanza Kunjufu, The Conspiracy to Destroy Black Boys, III (Chicago: African-American Images, 1990).

7. The Miami Herald, September 14, 1990

8. The Autobiography of Malcolm X, 262-263.

9. Mark Ridley-Thomas, "Time for a Progressive Attack on Drugs," Christianity and Crisis, September 11, 1989, 259-261; "The Muslims to the Rescue," Ebony, August 1989, 136-140; LAT, May 20, March

2, March14, 1990.

10. Ethan A. Nadelmann capsulizes the pros and cons of the decriminalization debate in "Challenge Is Not Whether to Decriminalize but How," LAT, March 20, 1990.

11. Louis Lieberman and Alexander B. Smith, "Crime Rates and Poverty--A Reexamination," Crime and Social Justice, No.25 (Summer, 1987) 172-173;

12. James DeFranzo, "Economic Assistance to Impoverished Americans," Criminology, Vol. 21, No.1 (February 1983) 126-127.

13. William Appleman Williams, *The Great Evasion* (Chicago: Quadrangle Books, 1964) 84-85.

14. The Urban League's Douglas Glasgow presents practical and workable social and economic policy reforms to attack the root cause of poverty and crime. All have been ignored by policy makers. *The Black Underclass*, 184-187. Also, Raymond J. Micholowski has developed some innovative ideas to reduce crime in, "Crime Control in the 1980's: A Progressive Agenda," Crime and Social Justice (Summer, 1983) 15-20.

CONCLUSION

1. WSJ, September 4, 1990.

RECOMMENDED READINGS

Bagdikian, Ben, *The Media Monopoly* (Boston: Beacon Press, 1987).

Banks, James A., and Grambs, Jean D., *Black Self-Concept* (New York McGraw-Hill, 1972).

Berry, Mary Frances, *Black Resistance/White Law* (New York Meredith Corp., 1971).

Clark, Ramsey, *Crime in America* (New York: Simon and Schuster 1970).

Collier, Christopher and Collier, James Lincoln, *Decision in Philadel phia* (New York: Ballantine Books, 1987).

Desmond, Dennis and Lusane, Clarence, *Stopping Bush's Drug Wai* (Washington, D.C.: Fighting Words Publication, 1990).

Flowers, Ronald Barri, *Minorities and Criminality* (Westport, Ct. Greenwood, 1988).

Franklin, John Hope, *From Slavery to Freedom* (New York: Vintage Press, 1969).

Frederickson, George M., *The Black Image in the White Mind* (New York: Harper & Row, 1971).

Garrow, David, *The FBI and Martin Luther King Jr.*, (New York: Penguin Books, 1983).

Gary Lawrence E. and Brown, Lee P., *Crime and its Impact on the Black Community* (Washington, D.C.: Howard University Press, 1975).

Ginsberg, Carl, *Race and the Media: The Enduring Life of the Moynihan Report* (New York: Institute of Media Analysis, Inc., 1989).

Glasgow, Douglas G., *The Black Underclass* (New York: Vintage Books, 1981).

Jenkin, Adelbert H., *The Psychology of the Afro-American* (New York: Pergamon Press, 1982).

Kunjufu, Jawanza, *The Conspiracy to Destroy Black Boys, III* (Chicago: African-American Images, 1990)

Langone, John, *The Causes of Violence* (New York: Little, Brown and Co., 1984).

Lefcourt, Robert, *Law Against the People* (New York: Vintage Press, 1971).

Lekachman, Robert, *Greed is Not Enough: Reaganomics* (New York: Pantheon, 1982).

Madhubuti, Haki R., *The Black Male: Obsolete, Single or Endangered?* (Chicago: Third World Press, 1990)

Malcolm X, *The Autobiography of Malcolm X* (New York: Grove Press, 1965).

National Urban League, *The State of Black America 1987* (New York: National Urban League, 1988).

O'Reilly, Kenneth, "Racial Matters": *The FBI's Secret File on Black America* (New York: Free Press, 1989)

Quinney, Richard, *Criminology: Analysis and Critique of Crime in America* (Boston: Little, Brown and Co., 1975).

Silberman, Charles E., *Criminal Violence, Criminal Justice* (New York: Vintage Press, 1976).

The State of Black American 1989 (New York:National Urban League 1989)

U.S. Department of Justice, "Report to the Nation on Crime and Justice "(Washington, D.C.: Government Printing Office, 1988).

Williams, Chancellor, *The Destruction of Black Civilization* (Chicago Third World Press, 1974).

Wilson, James Q. and Herrnstein, Richard J., *Crime and Human Nature* (New York: Simon and Schuster, 1985).

Wilson, William Junius, *The Declining Significance of Race in America* (Chicago: University of Chicago Press, 1978).

Wright, Kevin N., *The Great American Crime Myth* (New York Praeger, 1985)